SWEET PEAS
An essential guide

SWEET PEAS

An essential guide

Roger Parsons

THE CROWOOD PRESS

First published in 2011 by
The Crowood Press Ltd
Ramsbury, Marlborough
Wiltshire SN8 2HR

www.crowood.com

Revised paperback edition 2018

British Library Cataloguing-in-Publication Data
A catalogue record for this book is available from the British Library.

ISBN 978 1 78500 533 6

Frontispiece: Sweet Pea 'Ethel Grace' (S. Cuttle).

Typeset by Servis Filmsetting Ltd, Stockport, Cheshire
Printed and bound in India by Parksons Graphics

Contents

CARTERS NOVELTY 1935.

No.
P8864 **BLUE MOON.**— The best blue Sweet Pea we have ever raised, possessing an intensity of colour quite free from any reddish tinge (*see page 161*).　50 seeds, 2/6; 20 seeds, 1/-

CARTERS NOVELTY 1934

No.
P9482 **SUNRISE.** — The Gold Medal Variety.　Glowing clear cerise with a fleeting suggestion of orange, becoming more intense in the sun (*see page 161*). Per pkt., 1/-; extra large pkt., 2/6

CHAPTER 1

The early history of the Sweet Pea

Most readers will have picked up this book because they want to know how to grow better Sweet Peas. Some may think that the last thing they want is a 'boring old history lesson'. But in order to understand the plants that we grow today, it is helpful to have an understanding of how they originated and how they have developed. For many people, this will help them to decide the varieties that they want to grow, and such understanding adds to the satisfaction of growing Sweet Peas by placing them in a context.

For such a popular and well-known flower, it is surprising what nonsense has been written about the origins and early history of the Sweet Pea. These arose in the past from authors who have either failed to research the matter or did not have the benefit of modern science. Once speculation is presented in print as if it were fact, it appears to have some authority and the errors are perpetuated by later writers. The record was put right by the National Sweet Pea Society (NSPS) in its Centenary Celebration booklet, published in 2000. This included a fully referenced article on the history of the Sweet Pea, which is focused purely on historical evidence and follows considerable research. The article concludes that 'it is beyond doubt that the Sweet Pea originates in Sicily.'

ORIGINS OF THE SWEET PEA

The first reference to the Sweet Pea is by Franciscus Cupani in 1695 in his *Sillabus Plantarum Sicillae*. This was simply a list of names of plants newly

Nuper Detectarum from Carters' 1936 Catalogue.

SWEET PEA HAWLMARK PINK

Sweet Pea 'Hawlmark Pink', introduced in 1920.

Sweet Pea illustration by
Jan Mominckx in 1701.

discovered in Sicily. He first describes it in 1696 in his *Hortus Catholicus*. Plant names in those days were long descriptions in Latin and the name given by Cupani, to what in modern English we call the Sweet Pea, was *Lathyrus distoplatyphylos, hirsutus, mollis, magno et peramoeno, flore odoro*. Franciscus Cupani was born in 1657 and became a monk in 1681 at Palermo in Sicily. He had a broad interest in natural history and published several works before his death in 1711.

The earliest illustration of a Sweet Pea is in Casper Commelin's *Horti-Medici Amstelodamensis*, published in 1701 in the Netherlands, which he states was prepared from plants grown from seeds sent to him by Cupani in 1699. The artist is Jan Mominckx. It is believed that the Sweet Pea was introduced into England in 1699 when Cupani also sent seeds to Dr Robert Uvedale, a schoolmaster at Enfield, but there is no contemporary evidence for this. The original Sweet Pea was a 'purple' bicolour and is described by Leonard Plukenet in his *Almagesti Botanici Mantissa* of 1700. Dried specimens of Sweet Peas from Plukenet's herbarium are stored at the Natural History Museum in London.

Those who placed the origin of the Sweet Pea elsewhere often cited as evidence the fact that the Sweet Pea cannot be found growing in Sicily. This is remarkable since the collection of wild Sweet Peas from parts of Sicily and Southern Italy has been well documented over a long period. The first historian of the NSPS, S.B. Dicks, described how in 1896 he asked G. Sprenger, who was living in Naples, to visit Sicily and try to find the wild Sweet Pea. Sprenger found it in many parts and also in Sardinia. E.R. Janes noted in 1953 wild Sweet Peas having been seen in many of the Mediterranean islands, including Sicily. I maintain a stock of wild Sweet Peas sent by Dr Keith Hammett that were first collected from Sicily in 1974.

OTHER SPECULATION ON ORIGINS

Sri Lanka versus Sicily

The place having most claim to rival Sicily as the original source of the Sweet Pea is Sri Lanka, formerly known as Ceylon. This claim relied on a belief that the Sweet Pea was described from Ceylon earlier than Sicily, in part due to Johann Burmann's *Thesaurus Zeylanicus*, published in Amsterdam in 1737. Zeylana was an alternative form of Ceylon in use at the time. Burmann cites Hartog's herbarium as the source for *Lathyrus zeylanicus, hirsutus, flore angoate, odorato*. The word '*angoate*', meaning variegated, was used in the eighteenth century to describe pink and white bicoloured flowers while today it is most commonly associated with bicoloured foliage. From the Latin, Burmann says:

> Hartog or Hertog is a herbarium which I keep and which it is certain contains very many most elegant Zeylanian plants, and was sent once by him from Zeylana to Cornelius Voss the gardener at Leyden.

We do not have dates for Hartog's specimens and little is known about him. According to Linnaeus:

> John Hartog was born and trained for the service of Flora at the gardens of Leyden, at the time

Wild Sweet Pea collected from Sicily in 1974 (M. Thornhill).

Plukenet died in 1706, but in 1713 James Petiver describes the plants and says:

> This elegant sweet-flowered plant I first observed with Dr Plukenet in Dr Uvedale's most curious garden at Enfield, and since at Chelsea and elsewhere.

Plukenet's pressed specimen, photographed around 1908.

when the loss of Hermanus was being deplored by the whole world. William Sherard, who afterwards directed the Sceptre of Flora, was solicitous day and night regarding procuring the plants of Ceylon and publishing a brief description of them, and he frequently consulted a sincere friend, one celebrated by his learning, the well-known H. Boerhave.... Hartog was the only one willing to undertake a journey into Ceylon.

Paul Hermann or Hermanus lived from 1646 to 1695. William Sherard lived 1659–1728 and Herman Boerhave 1668–1739. The latter would not have had time to become celebrated much before 1700. In his *Index Plantarum* of 1710, Boerhave includes *Lathyrus siculus, flore odorato, ango* but there is no mention of a pink and white sweet pea, nor one from Ceylon. A later edition of 1720 lists:

Lathyrus distoplatyphyllos, hirsutus, mollis, ango et peramoeno, flore odoro Cupani Hort. Cath. H.A.2:159

Lathyrus siculus, flore odorato, ango Ind. 159.

There is again no reference to a pink and white Sweet Pea, nor one from Ceylon. The comprehensive lists of references in both editions make no mention of Hartog's collection.

Hartog did not return from Ceylon and, although he sent a herbarium, there is no evidence that he sent living seeds or plants from Ceylon. Burmann's description of *L. zeylanicus* appears to be based on an assumption that all the specimens in Hartog's herbarium, which he had received indirectly, came from Ceylon. An attempt in 1921 by S.B. Dicks to revisit the specimens in Hartog's herbarium found them no longer in existence. The only specimen in the Leyden herbarium labelled as *L. zeylanicus* proved to be another *Lathyrus* species, not *L. odoratus*.

Turning to more modern authors, the validity of Burmann's reference was challenged in the *Gardener's Chronicle* in 1900 and by Alvin Beal of Cornell University in 1912. There are several references which all confirm that botanists have been unable to find any wild Sweet Pea in Sri Lanka (Ceylon). Yet among later writers, E.R. Janes and Bernard Jones, the view that the Sweet Pea may have originated in Ceylon prevailed because of

ORIGIN OF THE NAME
LATHYRUS ODORATUS

When Linnaeus wrote his *Flora Zeylanica* of 1747, which is based on Hermann's herbarium, he made no reference to *L. zeylanicus*. However, in writing his comprehensive *Species Plantarum* of 1753, he could not ignore the existence in cultivation of the pink and white Sweet Pea. This work established the current binomial system of botanical names and for the first time gave the Sweet Pea the name we know today of *Lathyrus odoratus*. He describes two varieties of Sweet Pea: the purple form he named as *Lathyrus siculus*, which means from Sicily, and the pink and white bicolour he called *Lathyrus zeylanicus*, citing Burmann as the reference.

S.B. Dicks, who first researched the history of the Sweet Pea for the bicentenary celebration in 1900.

another reference suggesting the pink and white form pre-dates reference to the purple wild type.

Both James Justice and the great Victorian seedsman, Henry Eckford, thought the pink and white form was the original Sweet Pea, and the purple form was a variety of it. In 1754, James Justice says Bauhin listed the pink and white Sweet Pea as *Lathyrus angustifolius, flore ex albo et rubro variegate, odorato* in his *Historiae Plantarum* of 1650–1, written long before Hartog thought of going to Ceylon. This reference by Justice has been cited by authors ever since. However, my own direct reference to Bauhin's work, which contains extensive descriptions and references, shows no evidence of the name quoted by Justice. Bauhin describes a *Lathyrus flore rubro et alius albo* but nowhere is the key word *odorato* mentioned and there exist other *Lathyrus* species with pink and white bicoloured flowers e.g. *L. clymenum* var. *articulatus* (Arcangeli 1882); *L. vernus* var. *variegatus* (Bassler 1973).

These observations are supported by Boerhave who listed Bauhin's work as one of his references, yet the plant is not included in his *Index Plantarum*. Inclusion by Justice of the word *angustifolius*, meaning 'narrow-leaved', suggests he is not describing a Sweet Pea.

Before we leave Burmann, he also describes *L. zeylanicus, rubro pulcher* for which he cites Jacob Breyn's *Prodromus* of 1680 as a reference. There has been speculation that this is the first reference to a red Sweet Pea but it is significant that this was not picked up by other botanists and it is not clear that the plant described is scented.

Malta versus Sicily

Charles Unwin believed that the Sweet Pea originated from Malta on the assumption that the flower could be found growing wild there during his lifetime whereas he thought it had not been found growing in the wild in Sicily. John Borg's 1927 *Flora of Malta* describes eight *Lathyrus* species native to Malta but simply says of *L. odoratus*:

> The Sweet Pea is very frequently cultivated in gardens, and is often met with as a garden escape, but always dies out.

In 1974, Leonard Messel described the difficulties he was having growing Sweet Peas on Malta because of 'parasitic disease' in the soil. Unwin placed too much importance on the garden escapes he had seen growing in Malta and appears unaware of ample evidence of the Sweet Pea growing wild in Sicily.

South America versus Sicily

There are few parts of the world where the Sweet Pea has not been introduced and cultivated for its cut flowers, subsequently escaping to the wild and reverting to wild type. Some forms of wild Sweet Peas are called 'Quito' and 'Matucana' simply because that is where they were collected. Both were collected by Prof. S.C. Harland around 1955 and 'Quito' was specifically described as having been collected from a garden. 'Sicilian Pink', also known as 'Sicilian Fuchsia', was found growing in

Sweet Pea 'Matucana'.

the same spot in Peru as 'Matucana' and has no connection with Sicily. It was named by Harland in memory of Cupani. These are feral Sweet Peas which have become naturalized just as they have in many parts of the world to which Sweet Peas have been introduced.

In 1965, J.F. Turral speculated that the Spanish took the wild Sweet Pea to South America while the Portuguese took the pink and white form to Ceylon. He contended:

> it was the Moors in the Spanish peninsula, the best gardeners in mediaeval Europe, who developed it into a garden flower.

There is absolutely no evidence for involvement of the Moors and it is obvious from Turral's writing that this is wistful speculation. But it led Peter Grayson in the 1990s to place the introduction by the Moors into cultivation at around 1450 and by the Portuguese into Ceylon in 1520. These dates are a fantasy based on acceptance of Turral's speculation, although it is a nice idea to think that as invading armies marched across the mediaeval world, they made sure they took their prized Sweet Peas with them.

THE COLOUR OF THE FIRST SWEET PEA

What colour was Cupani's Sweet Pea? It is often described as 'purple', a description used by geneticists in the early part of the twentieth century to refer to what they quite clearly see as a bicolour. A 1939 paper states:

> The purple wild Sweet Pea has the wings much paler and bluer than the standard.

There are many 'wild type' Sweet Peas available at present which have a maroon standard and violet wings: the descriptions vary but the colour does not vary significantly! It is inevitable that the original Sweet Pea contained the dominant genes for all factors and these frequently arise as

Sweet Pea 'Cupani'.

throwbacks in seed batches. Grayson has suggested that Cupani selected and sent seeds of a more attractive form than the common wild type. The basis of this appears to be that the seeds sent in 1699 to Uvedale and Commelin were collected from plants grown by Cupani rather than plants growing in the wild. Varieties named 'Matucana' and 'Cupani' (or 'Cupani's Original') are often sold as being the original Sweet Pea introduced in 1699, or even earlier when the Spanish invaded South America. The size and vigour of these varieties shows that they are twentieth-century throwbacks. In the National Collection, there are several accessions of 'Matucana' and 'Cupani' and there is more variation within each variety than there is difference between them. One form of 'Matucana' has a length of raceme and number of flowers typical of Spencer origin. 'Cupani' has all the qualities of an Eckford grandiflora rather than anything more primitive. The stock of *L. odoratus* originally collected in the wild in 1974 is much less vigorous and is smaller in all parts than 'Matucana' or 'Cupani', usually having just two flowers per raceme.

White flowers

Speculation that the original Sweet Pea was pink and white has already been discussed since this is the colour form thought to have originated in Sri Lanka. Rev. W.T. Hutchins in America and Bernard Jones in Britain were among those who have speculated that a white variety may have been the forerunner of the other two colours. This appears to have been based on early references to white blooms in both *L. siculus* and *L. zeylanicus*. For example, H.B. Rupp, writing in 1718, says of the Sweet Pea:

Sometimes it varies with a white flower.

Our understanding of the genetics and distribution of the genus are now such that this claim cannot be accepted. The situation is best summed up by the words of R.C. Punnett in 1925:

The wild Sweet Pea, as it occurs today in Sicily, is a purple bicolour with erect standard.... These

experiments also shewed that we must regard the wild form as containing all the dominant characters hitherto recorded in the Sweet Pea, which is in accordance with the view that the cultivated forms have arisen by a series of losses of factors from type of the genetical constitution of the original wild species.

The genetic evidence supports the botanical and historical evidence of the Sweet Pea's origins in Sicily and nowhere else. The colour of this type is variously described around the theme of a maroon and violet bicolour.

EARLY CULTIVATION IN ENGLAND

It would be easy to create a fantasy about the Sweet Pea being grown in England prior to 1699

Sweet Pea 'Painted Lady' (C. Ball).

that has as little substance as some of the above claims. Perhaps it was introduced by the Romans along with the many plants that we know they introduced? Perhaps it was brought home by returning crusaders but subsequently lost? It is conceivable that someone in England grew seeds and either failed to harvest fresh seed for its continuation or discarded it in contempt of its lack of medicinal or culinary properties, its dull colouring, small flowers and weak racemes needing support. There is no evidence to support such speculation: these are merely imagination and should be dismissed.

We believe that the Sweet Pea was introduced into England in 1699 and it appears to have been grown continually ever since, starting with Petiver's account quoted earlier. In 1724, 'sweet sented pease' were offered for sale in his seed catalogue by Benjamin Townsend at the sign of the 'Three Crowns and Naked Boy', over against the new church in the Strand. (Pub names are just not as imaginative as they used to be.) In 1729, Henry Woodman of Chiswick, London sold 2oz. at 2 shillings.

Early mutations

The Sweet Pea's high propensity to mutate must have been evident from an early date as new colours arose. Beal attributes the earliest reference to the first variety named 'Painted Lady' to the first edition of Miller's work in 1731 but Dicks says it was the 1759 edition. The variety was simply another name for the pink and white form, *L. zeylanicus*, listed in 1737. We have also seen that the white form was known by 1718. Whatever records we have, in genetic terms, pink and white probably pre-dates white.

A catalogue of Robert Furber from the 1730s lists purple, white and 'variegated or Painted Lady sweet-scented pea.' In the eighteenth century, the flower was known to be variable from a very early time. Geneticists have shown that it only takes a single mutation in one factor to change the wild type flower colour into a pink and white bicolour. It takes just one more factor to be lost to change pink/white into pure white. Such changes have been observed in modern times. The white variety

'Bramdean' arose as a rogue in a previously fixed stock of a wild or feral variety collected at Anqua in Italy. There is no evidence of deliberate hybridization in the eighteenth century. Interesting mutations would have been selected and conserved and there may have been some accidental cross-pollination involved. By whatever means, slowly the number of varieties increased.

In 1775, Weston's *Flora Anglicana* lists *Lathyrus odoratus coccineus*, the 'Scarlet Sweet Pea.' Thomas Barnes of Leeds sold seed of scarlet, white, 'Painted Lady' and purple to Edwin Lascelles Esq. of Harewood in 1782. This was not the bright scarlet colour that we know today, but was a deep rose or carmine colour.

W. Curtis (1788) said:

> There is scarcely a plant more generally cultivated than the Sweet Pea.... Several varieties of this plant are enumerated by authors, but general cultivation extends to two only, the one with blossoms perfectly white, and the other white and rose-coloured, commonly called the Painted Lady Pea.

In 1793, a seedsman named John Mason of Fleet Street, London, catalogued and described five varieties: black, purple, scarlet, white and 'Painted

THE ORIGIN OF THE NAME 'SWEET PEA'

The references to the Sweet Pea by Weston and Curtis are also notable because for most of the eighteenth century they were known as Sweet Scented Peas. The first use of the common name shortened to Sweet Pea is frequently and incorrectly attributed to Keats.

Here are sweet peas, on tip-toe for a flight:
With wings of gentle flush o'er delicate white,
And taper fingers catching at all things,
To bind them all about with tiny rings.
From 'I stood tip-toe upon a little hill',
Keats 1816

Sweet Pea from *Curtis's Botanical Magazine*, 1788.

N.°60

Lady'. A 'black-purple' is mentioned in 1800, presumably the same as Mason's black. This is likely to be the drab form of wild type colour that can be seen for example in the variety 'Purple Prince' but may have been an early dark maroon. It would not be the dark maroon that is such a popular colour today. This did not exist a hundred years ago, when a common complaint about the dark maroon or black varieties was that they had too much 'purple' in them.

Sweet Pea 'Princess of Wales', introduced in 1885.

THE ADVANCE OF THE GRANDIFLORAS

Slowly the range of colours advanced. Martyn in 1807 describes the 'New Painted Lady' pea, with red standard and pink wings. A 'striped' Sweet Pea was first mentioned in 1817. The modern stripes first appeared in the 1920s. Prior to this, 'striped' flowers were what we now call 'flaked'. It was not until 1837 that the first flaked Sweet Pea appeared in commerce and it was with these that James Carter of Holborn, London, started a business

associated with the flower, continuing until well into the twentieth century. Carter also introduced the first 'yellow', as cream-coloured varieties have been called from time to time. Mrs Loudon's *Ladies' Flower Garden of Ornamental Plants* (1840) lists the purple wild type, 'New Painted Lady', 'Old Painted Lady', blue ('which has the wings and keel a pale blue and the standard dark bluish purple'), and violet ('which has the keel a pale violet, the wings a deep violet and the standard a dark reddish purple').

In 1860, a wire-edged variety was introduced by Carter but raised by Major Trevor Clarke and named 'Blue Edged'. It received a First Class Certificate (FCC) from the Royal Horticultural Society (RHS) in 1883 under the name 'Blue Hybrid' and was claimed by Clarke to be a hybrid between a white variety and Lord Anson's Pea, *L. nervosus*. It never bore any evidence of hybridity in vegetative parts and the claim must be regarded as spurious in the light of our current knowledge of the barriers to inter-specific hybridization in *Lathyrus*.

Although the colour range was increasing by the middle of the nineteenth century, there has been no indication that the habit and vigour of the plants was any different to the wild type, although it is reasonable to assume that some improvement may have taken place through unconscious or conscious selection. Mutation and accidental cross-pollination may have also played a role in this, providing improvements in vigour and capacity to photosynthesize which went unremarked. By small increments over many generations in the life cycle of an annual plant, some improvements can be expected. Between 1845 and 1849, Carter introduced 'New Striped' and 'New Large Purple' and this suggests that seedsmen had started to consciously improve the form and vigour of the plants.

Between 1860 and 1870, many new Sweet Peas were introduced, the result of increasing interest in the flower from commercial seedsmen in England and elsewhere in Europe. In 1867, 'Scarlet Invincible' became the first Sweet Pea to be recognized for award, receiving an FCC from the RHS. It was nearer carmine than a modern scarlet and remained popular for a long time. Varieties raised in Germany by Haage and Schmidt, such as 'Crown Princess of Prussia' and 'Fairy Queen', were introduced into Britain. But the range was still very limited and the old colour descriptions generally prevailed over variety names.

Sweet Pea mania arrives

After 1880, commercial interest in creating new Sweet Peas really went into overdrive from a wide variety of seedsmen, notably Henry Eckford and Thomas Laxton. From 1877, Thomas Laxton of Bedford began to improve Sweet Peas and in 1883, the same day Carter gained an FCC for 'Invincible Striped', Laxton secured a similar award for 'Invincible Carmine', said to be the result of crossing a red variety with a purple variety. 'Invincible Carmine' represents the earliest recorded result of cross-fertilization where the parents are known.

From 1883 onward, Laxton annually made many crosses. He produced many successful varieties. In addition, many of Laxton's crosses resulted in varieties that for all practical purposes were duplicates of those being put on the market by Henry Eckford but, according to Eckford's son:

Mr Laxton was too good a florist to create confusion by distributing similar varieties under different names and so his work was to a large extent discounted.

Henry Eckford was a tremendous self-publicist and is remembered as the father of the Sweet Pea. It is Henry Eckford whose name is most associated with the development of the Sweet Pea in the nineteenth century and who took it to its position as 'Queen of the Annuals'. Eckford was a head gardener at Sandywell, Gloucestershire, when he first took interest in hybridizing Sweet Peas and later moved to Boreatton Park in Shropshire. His first cultivar was 'Bronze Prince', very popular and of good form and colour, for which he secured his first certificate on 8 August 1882. But he had not yet learned the ability to fully fix varieties and it broke up. This was a useful lesson, for Eckford never subsequently released a variety unless it was fully fixed. His early introductions were distributed by others but he left private service and set up his own business at Wem, Shropshire. Eckford considered his introductions were such an

W. Atlee Burpee visits Henry Eckford at Wem, Shropshire.

improvement on those which had gone before that he coined the term 'grandiflora' to describe them. This name has stuck for all old-fashioned or pre-Spencer Sweet Peas. Grandifloras are discussed further in the next chapter. Eckford produced very many varieties, especially during the 1890s and right up to his death in 1906, when his business was continued by his son John.

THE BICENTENARY CELEBRATION OF 1900

There was by 1899 sufficient enthusiasm for Sweet Peas that the idea of celebrating the bicentenary of its introduction into England arose during an inspection of Sweet Peas at the trial grounds of Messrs Hurst and Sons in Kelvedon, Essex. The celebration consisted of an exhibition and conference held on 20–21 July 1900 at the Crystal Palace, London. Prior to this event, a meeting was arranged for 26 March 1900 by the bicentenary celebration organizing committee to create a London Sweet Pea Society. The meeting was invaded by Charles Curtis and Horace Wright who 'put up a great bluff' that a national society was in the process of being created and so those at the meeting formed the nucleus of the National Sweet Pea Society.

Charles Curtis and John Eckford presented a paper to the Bicentenary Celebration in which they state:

> From being such a small flower of not over vigorous habit, the Sweet Pea has been developed to a point at which we wonder where the next decided improvement will come.

They did not have to wait long. The new society, which remains very active to this day, organized its first exhibition of Sweet Peas at the Royal Aquarium, now the Methodist Central Hall, Westminster, on 25–26 July 1901. This was the occasion when Silas Cole, head gardener to Earl Spencer at Althorp, Northamptonshire, amazed everyone by displaying a bowl of pink Sweet Peas that were larger and frillier than anything that had previously been seen. They caused a sensation and were unanimously awarded a First Class

The only known picture of Sweet Pea 'Countess Spencer', taken in 1904.

Certificate. Cole named this new variety 'Countess Spencer' and large frilly Sweet Peas with an open keel have been known as Spencer type ever since.

THE EDWARDIAN ERA

The revolutionary variety 'Countess Spencer' is no longer with us; in fact only one picture of it exists. The story goes that the seedsman Robert Sydenham bought the variety and sent it to California for bulking up but when the seed crop returned, the variety had broken up. Charles Curtis was present at the time and referred to 'Countess Spencer' as a sport of 'Prima Donna'. Cole himself claimed to have created 'Countess Spencer' through hybridization but his account does not stand up to scrutiny by anyone with a simple understanding of the Mendelian inheritance that was then just becoming known to the world at large. Two other sports of 'Prima Donna' were reported at the same time, by Mr W.J. Unwin and by Henry Eckford.

On seeing 'Countess Spencer', W.J. Unwin exclaimed: 'I have that variety at home', but he did not release his form as 'Gladys Unwin' until 1904. It was 'a brighter, lighter rose pink colour than 'Countess Spencer''. Although considered a little less wavy than 'Countess Spencer', 'Gladys Unwin' had the distinct advantage of being completely fixed and its reliability meant that it was at first far more popular than 'Countess Spencer'.

The year following the introduction of Cole's 'Countess Spencer', Mr Eckford put on the market a stock of 'Countess Spencer' raised at Wem which was practically fixed – over 90 per cent of it came true and remained true. This was reported to have been bought by Eckford from a Mr Viner of Frome, Somerset, who had initially named it 'Nelly Viner'.

It seems extraordinary that such a startling new mutation could have arisen in three places at once. This has led some to pronounce divine intervention. There have been other instances of the apparently mysterious occurrence of significant new mutations in different places. Another example was the first dwarf variety 'Cupid' which was found in 1893 at Santa Clara, California, in a crop grown by C.C. Morse and Co. 'Cupid' had white flowers and arose as a sport in the white-flowered, tall-growing variety 'Emily Henderson.' Ernest Benary in Germany produced an identical variety at the same time and there were other reports of their existence. Does the Sweet Pea therefore have mystical qualities? It appears to me that in both these examples, mutation has occurred during the formation of a single seed pod and the seeds of that pod have been distributed widely to customers. Sadly we do not have enough information to confirm, for example, from where Cole, Unwin and Viner had obtained their seeds of 'Prima Donna'; or where Morse and Benary obtained their seeds of 'Emily Henderson'.

Cole introduced other Spencer varieties, sports of 'Countess Spencer'. From these and the Unwin and Eckford introductions, much hybridization took place as Edwardian Britain was seized by a frenzy of interest in Sweet Peas. In 1911, the *Daily Mail* newspaper organized a competition for the best bunch of Sweet Peas to be received by post and they received 39,000 entries from people hoping to win the £1,000 first prize, an enormous sum in those days. During the ten years up to 1914, the Spencer type, Unwin type and grandiflora type all vied with each other for popularity but it was the Spencer type that would emerge after the Great War on account of its longer racemes and bigger, more wavy flowers. The modern era of Sweet Pea growing was about to begin.

Sweet Pea 'White Cupid'.

CHAPTER 2

Types of Sweet Pea

The wonderful capacity for mutation displayed by the Sweet Pea has given modern gardeners a huge range of varieties from which to choose. My National Collection maintains around 1,000 varieties, each with their distinctive characteristics. In order to help us make sense of such diversity, humans like to categorize things. Frequently occurring forms of Sweet Pea have been grouped together as a 'type' to help us distinguish them from other forms. Any one named variety may in reality have characteristics from more than one of the types described below. Type names have also sometimes been used ambiguously in the past. The following remarks are therefore intended to help explain what is meant when these terms are encountered.

SPENCER TYPE

The Sweet Peas most commonly encountered have a Spencer flower form. By this, we mean that they have large blooms, frilly (sometimes called 'wavy') petals, and an open keel. The 'keel' is explained in Chapter 3. This Spencer form is so common that it is frequently found in early-flowering, multiflora, non-tendril, dwarf and intermediate varieties. So a reference to 'Spencer Sweet Peas' usually has a narrower definition and refers to the tall, summer-flowering varieties that are so popular with British and Irish gardeners because of their long racemes with large wavy blooms in a very wide range of colours – and, of course, their delightful scent.

The Spencer type originated from 'Countess

Sweet Pea 'White Supreme' (S. Cuttle).

Spencer', a variety first seen in 1901, and from similar varieties, such as 'Gladys Unwin'. When introduced, 'Countess Spencer' broke up into other colours and these became fixed, giving a small range of colours that could be crossed with each other to make new colour breaks. Further enlargement of the colour range was achieved in those early years by crossing with grandiflora varieties. Although Spencer flower characteristics are genetically recessive to the grandiflora type, a cross between a Spencer variety and a grandiflora variety should produce about 25 per cent of offspring with Spencer flower form.

Enhancement of the Spencer type

The Spencer type has been subject to intense hybridization during the twentieth century, which has led to varieties with significant hybrid vigour. On good soil, modern Spencer varieties can naturally grow to 2.1m (8ft) high and with excellent length of flower spikes. Much of this hybridization was driven by the demands of florists for cleaner, truer colours but it also caused a reduction in the range of colours available. Some colours found in early Spencer varieties were lost and, by the 1980s, most Spencer varieties available were self-coloured (i.e. all the petals were of uniform colour). Since then, considerable effort has gone into extending the range of colours. Pioneering work by the likes of Andrew Beane in Yorkshire and Keith Hammett in New Zealand, among others, means that the present-day gardener has a wonderful selection of varieties including those with striped, flaked and bicoloured flowers.

Modern Spencer varieties generally have four flowers per raceme (or flower spike) because

Sweet Pea 'Charlie's Angel'.

this is the optimum number favoured by flower show exhibitors. Most of the hybridizing in recent decades to produce new varieties has been carried out by amateur growers with exhibiting in mind, but ordinary gardeners who grow for cut flowers generally prefer five flowers. The emphasis on breeding new varieties for exhibition has also placed a greater emphasis on size of blooms. Really attractive and reliable varieties, with perfect formation but medium sized blooms, can often be overlooked.

Size and vigour of Spencer type

It is generally considered that Spencer Sweet Peas are becoming altogether bigger as a result of intense hybridization. For example, in flower size, the best exhibition variety in a particular colour nowadays may have a standard that is 60mm across when fifty years ago the best exhibition variety in the same colour would have had a 55mm standard. In the 1920s, the equivalent variety would have had a 50mm standard. The opposite occurs in older varieties. A variety that was 55mm across when

Spencer blooms grown naturally up netting. The variety is 'Naomi Nazareth'.

first introduced will lose hybrid vigour during decades of generations of seed production so that nowadays the same variety will be only 45–50mm across. It is not just flower size that is affected. Vigour of plant, length of flower spike and size of leaf are also affected. With this is a perception among older growers that modern varieties do not retain this exceptional vigour for as long. Leading varieties in their day, such as 'Leamington', would be at their best for a longer period. We now have a lot of Spencer varieties introduced each year that are identical in colour to an existing variety and only time spent growing them can tell whether or not they are an improvement.

GRANDIFLORA TYPE

The term 'grandiflora' was coined by Henry Eckford for his varieties to show they were bigger and better than any Sweet Peas that had previously been seen. It is therefore ironic that 'grandiflora' varieties are nowadays smaller than the Sweet Peas that people most commonly encounter. The name is therefore misleading and other attempts to define the type have been made. The term 'pre-Spencer' is sometimes encountered in order to indicate that these varieties are the small flowers with plain petals and a clamped keel, the only type known prior to the advent of the Spencer type. Objections to the term pre-Spencer have arisen because many of the existing grandiflora varieties were introduced later than 1901. In other words, the flower form may be pre-Spencer but the varieties themselves are not. An alternative term used to overcome this problem is 'old-fashioned', suggesting the varieties are of old-fashioned type, even if they are of modern origin. Some seedsmen have introduced their own terms to cover this group of varieties, including Heritage, Heirloom and Antique. However, 'old-fashioned' is the term adopted by the National Sweet Pea Society and is therefore preferred.

Grandiflora as a flower form

There is another sense in which the term 'grandiflora' is used and this refers to any flower spike

Sweet Pea 'Henry Eckford'.

that has plain petals and a clamped keel. It is quite common for Spencer varieties to revert to grandiflora type; so that the flower spikes may have all the size and vigour of the Spencer variety but the individual flowers are plain and have a clamped keel. The problem arises because of the Sweet Pea's propensity for mutation. It starts with just one plant in a field of a variety being grown for seed reverting to grandiflora flower form. Large scale production of seed allows for the removal of 'rogue' plants that are the wrong colour but it does not allow for the removal of plants that are the right colour but the wrong form. Genetically, the grandiflora form is dominant to the Spencer form and it is also more fecund (i.e. produces more seed) so that over several generations the proportion of plants of grandiflora form will increase. After a couple of decades, the form of the crop may have become entirely grandiflora.

EXAMPLE OF REVERSION IN SPENCER TYPE

I was recently judging a class for white or cream varieties at a Sweet Pea show. One vase put up by a novice exhibitor was labelled 'Swan Lake', a variety that I had not seen on the show bench for decades and was obviously purchased from a non-specialist seedsman. Now 'Swan Lake' was a wonderfully frilly variety and very popular with exhibitors in the 1960s. But the blooms in this vase were entirely of grandiflora form and therefore were not really 'Swan Lake'. It is a common problem for me when trying to conserve old varieties. I may receive stock of an old variety which was thought to have been lost and on growing it find that most if not all the plants have lost their original Spencer character.

Size and vigour of grandiflora type

Just how big were Eckford's grandifloras compared with their predecessors? We cannot know precisely because there are few records and flower size is dependent on how well the plants have been grown. S.B. Dicks measured Plukenet's dried specimen that had been pressed in 1700 and found the width to be 1⅜ inches (35mm). You will find the same measurement from plants of the wild Sweet Pea stock originally collected in Sicily in

1974. Charles Curtis and John Eckford, writing in 1900, stated that '1⅗ inches in breadth can be secured under good cultivation in the newer Eckford forms.' This would be 40mm, a similar size to that found nowadays in the same varieties. It might be expected that a hundred or more years of seed generations would have led to the surviving Eckford varieties being smaller than they were when first introduced but this appears not to be the case.

In terms of vigour, nowadays an Eckford variety grown naturally will make up to 1.8m (6ft) high, more in a polytunnel. Denholm Fraser, writing in 1911, said that twenty or thirty years previously, a row of Sweet Peas would have formed a short hedge 3 or 4 feet high (0.9–1.2m) in a limited range of colours but by 1911 could be 8 or 10 feet high (2.1–3.0m). Perhaps some of their vigour has been lost in the past hundred years but I think it is more likely that Fraser's measurements were prone to exaggeration. He claimed his Spencer varieties were 2½ inches (over 60mm) across, which would make them as large as the latest modern varieties.

One other improvement during the Eckford period (for we must not forget the many other hybridizers working on Sweet Peas) was the number of flowers per raceme. By 1900, well-grown plants of the newer varieties might have 50 per cent of racemes containing four flowers, when in older times three flowers was the maximum and two was acceptable. The variety 'Queen Alexandra', introduced in 1906, then and now often produces only two flowers but was an award-winning introduction as the first truly sunproof scarlet.

Authenticity of old-fashioned varieties

In terms of flower size, vigour and number of flowers, we can be fairly confident that the old-fashioned varieties grown today are more or less the same as they would have been when first introduced. That does not mean that all such varieties on sale are as authentic as they purport to be. Some have been continually grown for the past 100 years, maintained by a very few enthusiasts, and occasionally making an appearance at

A group of 'Painted Lady' (C. Ball).

an exhibition of the National Sweet Pea Society. By the middle of the twentieth century they had virtually died out and those known to exist at the time were documented in detail by J.F. Turral in 1965. These seed lines were passed on by Turral's widow to Keith Hammett who has maintained them in his seed bank for decades and I now have these authentic lines back on sale to the general public. Renewed interest in old-fashioned varieties has also led in the past twenty years to the 'rediscovery' of varieties that have been given the name of an older variety but are modern creations of old-fashioned type. An example of this is 'Blanche Ferry'. This was discovered as a tall-growing rogue in 'Pink Cupid' by Ron Bailey and reintroduced by him in 1990. However the notable feature of 'Blanche Ferry' was that it is early flowering, yet this stock is not early. There may however be a genuine stock of 'Blanche Ferry', perhaps conserved in the USA, but I have yet to see it. In too many varieties the authenticity is not known or doubtful.

Sweet Pea 'Prima Donna'.

EARLY-FLOWERING TYPES

Most Sweet Pea varieties are summer-flowering. The factors that lead to flowers forming are not exclusively based on day-length but this is a significant feature of the early-flowering types. Summer-flowering varieties appear to require twelve hours of daylight before they will initiate flower production but the early-flowering types will flower on shorter day lengths. I have used the word 'types' rather than 'type' deliberately because they are also described as 'spring-flowering' or 'winter-flowering'. As a general rule, the spring-flowering type requires eleven hours of daylight and the winter-flowering type requires ten hours to initiate flowering. In practice, early-flowering varieties are usually available within a 'series' and, although a series may be described as winter-flowering

or spring-flowering, in practice the day length required may be intermediate. In other words, some winter-flowering varieties may be earlier than others. It is also evident that some series are more homogeneous than others, the worst having varying day length within the series.

Few grow early-flowering types within the UK apart from commercial cut flower growers. Spring-flowering varieties may be grown outdoors in favoured parts of the UK but otherwise they are too badly damaged by weather to be worthwhile. The main benefit in the UK is when early types are grown in heated glasshouses or polytunnels so that early blooms can be achieved, which attract a good price as cut flowers. The earliest winter varieties will generally start flowering in mid February on the south coast of England but other factors affect flower initiation so that I have known them start as early as late November and as late as mid-March.

Popularity around the world

Early types may not be very popular in the UK but for most of the world they are the preferred type to grow. This is because their earlier flowering allows the blooms to flourish at a cooler time of the year in climates where summer-flowering plants would

LEFT: Sweet Pea 'Oyama Russian Blue'.

ABOVE: Sweet Pea show held in a Japanese shopping mall (K. Nakamura).

wither in hot daytime temperatures. So for much of the USA, Japan, Australia and southern Europe, among others, early-flowering varieties are the types that are most popular.

The early-flowering character was first recorded in 'Blanche Ferry', introduced in the USA by D.M. Ferry in 1889. This arose from unconscious selection of 'Painted Lady' by a quarryman's wife over forty years when saving only the earliest seeds each year. This was used by hybridists to produce a number of pioneering series. Some of these have long been lost, such as those developed in Algiers by the Rev. Edwyn Arkwright and in the UK by C. Englemann. Much development of this type has taken place in the USA. For example, Anton Zvolanek grew cut flowers for market and one year noticed a plant in a row of 'Lottie Eckford' which was two weeks earlier than the others. He saved seed from this plant and crossed it with 'Blanche Ferry'. Subsequent generations produced many variations in flowering date but from these he selected 'Zvolanek's Christmas', introduced in

1899. In 1902, he received seeds of 'Countess Spencer' and many more crosses led to Zvolanek's Early Flowering Spencer series. In 1907, Lester Morse noted these as:

> really a distinct class. Planted in October they give cut flowers all winter, and until the following June. The stems are long and the blossoms of fine size – unquestionably useful for greenhouse work.

Spencer Praecox varieties

Many more winter-flowering varieties with Spencer flower form were developed in the USA during the first half of the twentieth century until their popularity was overtaken by the early multiflora type. Some of these still exist and are known, particularly to Dutch growers, as Spencer Praecox type in order to distinguish them from the early multiflora type. We maintain some of these in the National Collection, and have them available for

Sweet Pea 'Ronnie'.

sale, though often find that old varieties sent in have reverted to grandiflora or semi-grandiflora flower type and sometimes they are beyond re-selection. They have not yet all been grown but the best include 'American Beauty' (crimson), 'Elizabeth' (rose pink on white ground) and 'Pearl Buck' (orange pink/deep rose bicolour).

A popular spring-flowering type is the Cuthbertson series. In 1930, Frank Cuthbertson of the Ferry Morse Co. selected a particularly strong and vigorous plant which also produced extra long racemes. The colour was poor but it produced a mixture of colours, mostly of vigorous growth. He selected the best of these and crossed them with early-flowering varieties to obtain a wide range of colours, the first of which were intro-duced in 1940. They flower three weeks earlier than summer types in California but this margin is reduced to one week in the UK. They also have an element of the heat resistance so necessary for success in America. The name 'Cuthbertson' has now become confused with the spring-flower-ing type generally and includes the Cuthbertson Floribunda series, a multiflora series devel-oped by crossing Cuthbertsons with Zvolanek's Multifloras. An improved series, known as Royal series, was released by Ferry Morse in 1965. Quality of Cuthbertson varieties differs depending where they have been maintained. We have good stocks of 'Frank G.' (lavender), 'Lois' (rose pink on cream ground), 'Ronnie' (orange) and 'Royal Maroon' (dark maroon), among others still to try.

Australian Sweet Peas

In Australia, a winter-flowering variety, having flowers with Spencer form, is recorded in 1909. It was found in the Sydney garden of James Young and was named 'Yarrawa'. It had a bright rose standard with paler wings and apparently bred true in the first generation. 'Yarrawa' was an immensely successful variety, being used by hybridists in Australia and the USA to produce improved vari-eties of winter-flowering type. There appears to have been more swapping of material between these two countries in the first few decades of the twentieth century but after the 1940s Australian growers appear to have become more introverted,

Sweet Pea 'Christine Martin'.

hybridizing in isolation to the rest of the world. A benefit of this is that distinct series appeared with interesting characteristics, but sadly most of these have now been lost. It appears that only the Gawler series remains, being actively maintained and protected by the McDougall family in South Australia.

GAWLER SWEET PEAS

Gawler varieties frequently have distinct characteristics such as smooth (or hairless) vegetative parts and seed pods, duplex and triplex standards and the most delicious scent. They also have some unusual colours that have now been used in crosses with Spencer varieties to widen the range of fancy-coloured Spencers. It has been suggested Gawler series are a distinct type because of their unusual features but equally some Gawler varieties are hard to distinguish from Spencer Praecox varieties. With me, Gawler varieties are generally among the earliest to flower but flower spikes contain only two or three flowers in the UK. This number does not increase until later in the spring when fours can sometimes be achieved. The best with me of those tried so far include 'Christine Martin' (lilac pink on cream ground), 'Gawler Margaret' (lavender blue flake on white ground), 'Marilyn Jean' (mid blue), 'Natalie Joy' (dark blue) and 'Thelma May' (deep violet). 'Don Mac' has the best colour in any dark maroon of any type of Sweet Pea.

Japan

Commercial cut flower production of Sweet Peas is taken very seriously in Japan where the market remains buoyant by western standards. Their season is November to April so winter types are preferred. Japanese growers are very protective of their varieties and as a result of this they have maintained good stocks of Spencer Praecox varieties. Many of this type in my National Collection have come from Japan thanks to the generous support of Keith Hammett. There is also some hybridization carried out in Japan but varieties arising are not shared with other growers, especially not competitors in Japan. The long-term benefit of this isolation is that distinct types can be developed to suit local conditions. The risk is that there is currently no backup storage in a seed bank, so genetically distinct material could be lost, as occurred in Australia.

Sweet Pea 'Megumi Orange' (K. Nakamura).

Sweet Pea 'Ben-Shikibu' growing in Japan (K. Nakamura).

Sweet Pea 'Misora' (K. Nakamura).

MULTIFLORA TYPE

Multiflora Sweet Peas are those with more than five flowers per raceme. They can be found as summer-flowering varieties or early-flowering varieties. The first multiflora variety is considered to have been 'Sextet Queen', introduced by Suttons around 1930. This was a white flowered variety, making it very suitable for crossing with other colours, and other varieties with a 'Sextet' prefix were introduced by Suttons during the 1930s. In its first few seasons, 'Sextet Queen' was popular for exhibition because it retained all six flowers fresh at the same time. This character was lost and did not reappear in later varieties. Flower size also quickly reduced so that the type lost favour.

The next significant step for summer-flowering multifloras was the introduction by Burpee Seeds in 1958 of their Galaxy series, presumably created by crossing early multiflora varieties with Spencer varieties. These produced up to eight flowers per raceme. They are still available as a mixture, although in my experience have reverted to lose their multiflora character. In the 1990s, Denholm introduced the Bouquet series and these had a brief spell in commerce in the UK. They remain available as a mixture in the USA and have their supporters.

Early multiflora varieties

Across the Atlantic, in 1947, William Zvolanek, son of Anton, selected a plant with six flowers per raceme among 'Early Zvolanek Rose'. After many crosses, he produced a hybrid which usually produced six to eight flowers, sometimes eleven on long racemes. His first commercial variety was 'Whirlwind' and other early multifloras soon appeared. These early multiflora varieties had poor placement of flowers along the raceme and relatively small flowers. An improved type appeared in 1960 when Denholm introduced their Early Multiflora Gigantea series, some of which still exist. These proved extremely popular with cut flower growers in many parts of the world. They have been periodically renewed by reselection and crossing. In 1973, David Lemon joined Denholm Seeds and started working on them, creating the

A multiflora grandiflora seedling raised by Keith Hammett.

Mammoth series introduced in 1982. In 1984, David moved to Bodger Seeds where he created the Winter Elegance series introduced in 1992. David has continued to work on this type, producing the material refined for the UK and introduced by Owls Acre as Winter Sunshine series. His latest evolution is Solstice series which is not yet widely available because of poor seed harvests.

Multiflora varieties have been used by Keith Hammett as part of his breeding programme using *L. belinensis* × *L.odoratus* material. I have grown some of these and was impressed by their raceme length and long flowering period. Some have grandiflora flower form but whether there is a market for 'multiflora grandifloras' remains to be seen. They may prove very useful to hybridizers.

SEMI-GRANDIFLORA TYPE

We have already noted that varieties with a Spencer flower form have wavy petals and an open keel while those of grandiflora form have plain petals and a clamped keel. Plants with intermediate characters have long been observed but usually dismissed by hybridists. The most frequently observed form is when flowers have wavy petals and a clamped keel. This was known by the 1920s as the semi-grandiflora type. As with the term 'grandiflora', it does not seem entirely appropriate in a modern context but nobody has yet come up with a better name.

Plants are occasionally seen which are an intermediate type with plain petals and an open keel but there is no value in trying to fix these as a variety. However, the semi-grandiflora type have started to become popular in the UK in recent years and the NSPS has introduced a class for

Sweet Pea 'Albutt Blue'.

them at its exhibitions. The first of these was 'Albutt Blue', introduced by Eagle in 1999. It was raised by the late Harvey Albutt who was trying to create a blue picotee Spencer variety working from grandiflora material. 'Albutt Blue' is a truly superb variety, having the most delicious scent and with delightful wavy petals, white in colour but with a distinct blue picotee edge. Harvey did not quite achieve his goal because the variety has a clamped keel, making it as prolific to produce seed as the grandiflora type. The flowers are not quite as large as a modern Spencer and the racemes not quite as long but they are more than adequate, meaning that the variety has become popular with some cut flower growers. Other semi-grandiflora varieties are now also available but these have often arisen through reversion of Spencer varieties rather than deliberate crossing to produce them. Those who complain that modern Sweet Peas do not have the scent of the old ones simply need to grow 'Albutt Blue'.

SNAPDRAGON TYPE

It would have been very easy until recently to dismiss the Snapdragon type of Sweet Pea as an historical curiosity not worth mentioning in a book at this time. The name arises from extreme hooding of the standard petal to create a flower similar to a Snapdragon, or *Antirrhinum*. In 1897, the Sunset Seed and Plant Co. of California introduced 'Red Riding Hood', the first of the Snapdragon series. Other introductions followed over the next five years but the series was never popular. They died out within ten years. Frank Cuthbertson said of them:

> The standard… is undeveloped and forms a cap or hood over the wings. Wings… are partially gathered under the standard.

And that might have been the end of the story except that in 2003 Peter Grayson introduced a variety named 'Lady's Bonnet' of similar form. This variety is of old-fashioned type with mid-blue petals. The mutation may not be exactly the same as the Snapdragon type but 'Lady's Bonnet'

'Snapdragon' flower form, showing how the standard folds down to envelop the wings and keel.

nonetheless has a malformed and extremely hooded standard. Then in 2009 I was sent some pictures of a flower show at Miyazaki prefecture in southern Japan. Among all the other Sweet Peas were vases of Snapdragon Sweet Peas, one vase of pink flowers and one of white. Apparently the mutation arose there in 'Stella', which is an early multiflora variety with cream flowers, and has been presumably crossed with other varieties to widen the colour range. It appears that this mutation is exactly the same as the original Snapdragons but they remain primarily a botanical curiosity.

NON-TENDRIL TYPE

The non-tendril type is also sometimes known as acacia-leaved. They have a more primitive leaf form than most Sweet Peas in that the leaves have more than one pair of leaflets. Most Sweet Peas have a single pair of leaflets because the other leaflets are reduced to tendrils, an adaptation that allows the plant to climb. The practical effect of the non-tendril type is that leaves have a larger surface area for photosynthesis but the plants need to be tied to a support for climbing.

Tall non-tendril Sweet Peas have been known since about 1889 but originally had rather weak racemes and poor flowers. George Burt produced a series of tall non-tendril varieties with Spencer flower form for E.W. King and Co. during the 1930s and 1940s. Harvey Albutt and Dick Place, both sadly now dead, have produced modern varieties of this type which are occasionally encountered.

Plant with multijugate or non-tendril leaf form.

I recently grew some of these and found the quality good enough for exhibition. They have the obvious advantage to cordon growers that removal of tendrils is not necessary but there are too many leaves when it comes to lowering. They need more tying in when grown naturally.

More commonly encountered are dwarf varieties with non-tendril leaves. These derive from work done by Jim Tandy for E.W. King and Co. In 1957, he crossed George Burt's tall non-tendril hybrids with the Spencer 'Geranium Pink Improved' in order to increase their flower size to contemporary standards. By 1962, he was able to cross the resulting progeny with Zvolanek's Pygmy series. Following much crossing, back-crossing and selection, he produced a dwarf non-tendril series known as the Snoopea series, fully introduced in 1980. Supersnoop series and Explorer series are later evolutions of this material. They can usually only be bought as mixtures.

DWARF AND INTERMEDIATE-HEIGHT TYPES

Dwarfness in Sweet Peas is controlled by a simple recessive gene and it seems likely, as with early flowering and non-tendril leaves, that the character must have appeared many times in the past. It was only during the heightened interest in raising new Sweet Pea varieties at the end of the Victorian era that the character was selected and fixed.

Cupid varieties

The white-flowered 'Cupid' first appeared in 1893 with C.C. Morse and Co. in a crop of 'Emily Henderson', a tall white. It bred true and by 1895, Morse was able to grow 7 acres (2.9 hectares) of 'Cupid' for introduction in 1896. W. Atlee Burpee had purchased the variety in 1894 and had it grown in England by James Douglas. It was exhibited in 1895 when it was given two Awards of Merit, one by the Royal Horticultural Society and the other by the National Horticultural Society of France. Just as the Spencer break occurred in the same year in several places, so Ernest Benary in Germany was able to select a dwarf white

Sweet Pea 'Pink Cupid'.

which he was about to release as 'Tom Thumb White' until Burpee published details first. In 1895, similar dwarfs appeared in France and with Henry Eckford in England.

'Pink Cupid' appeared among 'Blanche Ferry' in 1895 and Burpee reported that he paid $1,500 for the stock of 1,068 seeds before introducing it in 1898. Where 'Cupid' had pale seeds that had a reputation for poor germination in unfavourable seasons, 'Pink Cupid' has dark seeds and remains available to this day. In 1897, the white produced a cream-coloured sport, 'Primrose Cupid'. These three colours were crossed with one another and with taller varieties, of both grandiflora and Spencer flower form, to produce the original of all dwarf types. In 1916, Frank Cuthbertson listed twenty-nine dwarf varieties.

Little Sweetheart series have Spencer flower form. Many dwarf types were developed around the 1960s, particularly in North America. Little Sweetheart series is now largely superseded by Burpee's Patio series. With me, Patio series and Bijou series are early flowering. Bijou series was introduced by Burpee in 1962, the result of crosses between dwarf seedlings and Galaxy series, to produce a dwarf multiflora series. As with Galaxy, nowadays Bijou series appears to have lost this multiflora character.

CUPID SWEET PEAS TODAY

Cupid series remains the most frequently encountered dwarf Sweet Pea and it is sometimes possible to buy these as individual colours rather than simply as a mixture. They are sold under a range of different trade names, such as Cherub series, Fantasia series, Pinocchio series and Sweetie series, but are all essentially the same with a grandiflora flower form. Some include fancy coloured varieties bred by Andrew Beane in the 1990s. Cherub series includes material produced by Owls Acre in the twenty-first century and is said to be better suited to the UK climate.

Intermediate height

Although the genetic relationship between tall and dwarf Sweet Peas can be simply demonstrated, there are also different series that have arisen which are intermediate in height. Bateson referred to these as 'bush' type in his 1909 book on Mendel's Principles of Heredity. The origins of this bush type are obscure but the controlling gene affects whether growth is determinate (i.e. reaches a certain height and then only side shoots are formed) or indeterminate (i.e. just keeps extending). All tall-growing Sweet Peas are indeterminate. The actual height of an intermediate variety will vary depending how well it is grown but dwarf ones are fairly consistently around 30cm (1ft). Knee-hi series resulted from crosses between Zvolanek's Pygmy series and Cuthbertson varieties and, again, were originally multiflora. They grow to 1m (3ft 4in) high if supported and were introduced by Ferry Morse. Jet-Set series arose from crosses between Knee-hi series and Royal series. Snoopea series and Supersnoop series, discussed in the previous section, should also be considered as intermediate rather than fully dwarf.

Cultivation of determinate varieties

All dwarf and intermediate types are best grown in a hot sunny position; so have never been as popular in the UK as in the USA. Try growing them in pots so that they can be moved around according to prevailing weather conditions. For seed production, they grow well in a well-ventilated polytunnel. Their reluctance to set seed outdoors in the UK makes them usable as a bedding plant because there is a lower requirement to remove dead flower heads. Intermediate forms benefit from some sort of support while the dwarf ones can just be left to trail if preferred. Cupid series have recently been marketed in the UK as trailing varieties suitable for hanging baskets and containers. You can also tie them into a short cane so that they have a more upright flower form. Bateson also illustrated what he called an 'erect cupid' type of Sweet Pea, arising from crossing the bush type with Cupids. This gave some offspring with trailing (i.e. Cupid) growth habit and some very dwarf plants with a

'Jet Set' and 'Explorer' intermediate height series on trial at Wisley Gardens.

more erect habit. This erect cupid type are only found in the historical record but they appear to have the potential to make better garden plants than Cupids. Keith Hammett reports having identified plants of this habit growing among a field crop of Cupids in Tasmania and has now secured seed of these but it may be a long time before we find them in general cultivation.

DUPLEX AND TRIPLEX FLOWERS

We cannot be certain when or where the first Sweet Pea with a double standard appeared but Walter Wright, writing in 1912, stated:

> I have no recollection of seeing duplication in a plain-type variety, but I should hesitate to say that it never appeared. Double standards soon began to come in the Spencers, and it was noticed that they were most abundant in the very vigorous sorts....

However, Alvin Beal (1914) said of 'Bride of Niagara', introduced by Vick in 1896:

> The flowers often had two or three banners.

(Banner is the term used in North America for the standard.)

Duplex standards were not welcomed by the majority of Sweet Pea lovers since they robbed the flower of its symmetry. They were, however, welcomed by commercial cut flower growers who saw this as a step towards fully double flowers. Double flowers in other species of flower, such as Stock, *Aster* and *Zinnia*, generally travel and last better than single forms but perfect doubleness comes when all parts of the flower, including the pistil and stamens, become petals. This causes a problem for seedsmen as they are sterile, so strains need to be produced which are fertile but produce a high proportion of double flowers. The potential increase in commercial cut flower production, if

Sweet Pea 'Linda Mary' showing duplex flower form.

what we now call 'vase life' of cut Sweet Peas could be increased, was a tremendous incentive to Sweet Pea breeders at the start of the twentieth century. The term 'duplex' to refer to double standards was coined by one of them, W. Atlee Burpee of Philadelphia, USA. Although not favoured by the amateur gardener and Sweet Pea exhibitor in the UK, duplex flowers had their champions and new varieties with this character still appear from time to time. It is easy for the present-day enthusiast to bemoan the fact that older varieties have become malformed and contain a proportion of duplex flowers which cannot be selected out, when in fact the variety was probably selected by its raiser for this characteristic.

The characteristic was associated with extreme waviness and seen as an evolution towards even more waviness which might end up in a ball of frill replacing each flower. 'Fluffy Ruffles' was a very frilly, rosy cream pink which often produced duplex flowers and was the first of what became popular in North America as the Ruffled series.

Although frilly, this series was slightly short in the raceme. The introduction by Robert Bolton of 'Gigantic' in 1934 with huge, densely frilled blooms, often duplex, has had a major impact on the production of modern varieties because of its many outstanding characteristics, not just frilliness. This has led to many introductions having the duplex character, or even triplex flowers containing three standards. Many Gawler varieties also display duplex and triplex standards.

The term 'duplex flowers' should not be confused with twin flowers arising from a single axil (explained in the next chapter). Experienced growers will have seen this phenomenon from time to time. Around 1970, Unwins released a selection of 'Leamington', which was twin-stemmed. It was used as a parent with other varieties but interest appears to have fizzled out. The very attractive intermediate height variety 'Balcony Bride', introduced around 1998, is very unusual in having twin flowers.

CHAPTER 3

Understanding how Sweet Peas grow

The first two chapters have explained the history and development of the Sweet Pea up to the present time. This chapter describes the Sweet Pea as we know it today. So we start by defining what a Sweet Pea is and how it grows. This leads us into an exploration of how we can manipulate these qualities for our own benefit. The detailed chapters on growing Sweet Peas that follow will rely on a basic understanding of the plants and their life cycle arising from this current chapter.

WHAT IS A SWEET PEA?

The Sweet Pea, known botanically as *Lathyrus odoratus*, is a distinct and clearly defined species. It does not readily hybridize with other *Lathyrus* species and all the many flower colours and different types of Sweet Pea have arisen through mutation and hybridization within the single species. Hybridization with other *Lathyrus* species is unknown in the wild and attempts by plant breeders to cross with other *Lathyrus* species have been unsuccessful. Only in recent years has hybridization taken place using laboratory techniques such as 'embryo rescue'. Hybrids have been induced with *L. hirsutus* and with *L. belinensis*, but hybrid material always segregates during several generations to the characteristics of one or other parent.

Botanical description

The Sweet Pea, *L. odoratus*, always has an annual life cycle. Popular references to the 'perennial

Sweet Pea 'Jacqueline Ann' (S. Cuttle).

sweet pea' refer to another species, invariably *Lathyrus latifolius*. In the Sweet Pea, the root system is fibrous. Vegetative parts, collectively known as haulm, are normally hairy but some Gawler varieties display hairless, sometimes called smooth, characteristics. Growing stems are upright and vigorous, climbing to 2.1m (8 feet) or more, but dwarf and bush forms exist. The stem is strongly winged i.e. it has flat, leaf-like tissue along and on opposite sides of it. Leaves are paripinnate (*see* Glossary, page 187) in shape and arise alternately along the stem at nodes. At each node is a stipule which is semi-sagittate in shape. Each leaf consists of a winged petiole about 3–4.5cm (1½in) long, and mid-rib with leaflets more or less opposite. The leaflets are generally seen as a single pair (unijugate) with other leaflets reduced to form branched tendrils. Non-tendril types retain all their leaflets (multijugate) and can be up to 25cm (10in) long. Each leaflet is ovate-elliptic in shape and has pinnate veins. Leaflet size varies enormously with type and with method of cultivation but is around 1.5 times longer than the width. Side growths and racemes are produced in the leaf axil, sometimes called axillary growths.

The flower stem is a raceme containing two to eleven or more flowers on one side, and varies considerably in length according to type and method of cultivation. Each flower arises on a pedicel at the end of a peduncle and is held within a calyx that opens to display teeth of equal length, 7–8mm (just over ¼in). The flowers are sweetly scented, 3–6cm across. Each flower classically consists of five petals: an upright petal, named a vexillum but usually called a standard or banner in allusion to its flag-like appearance, which is stenonychioid (*see* Glossary, page 187)

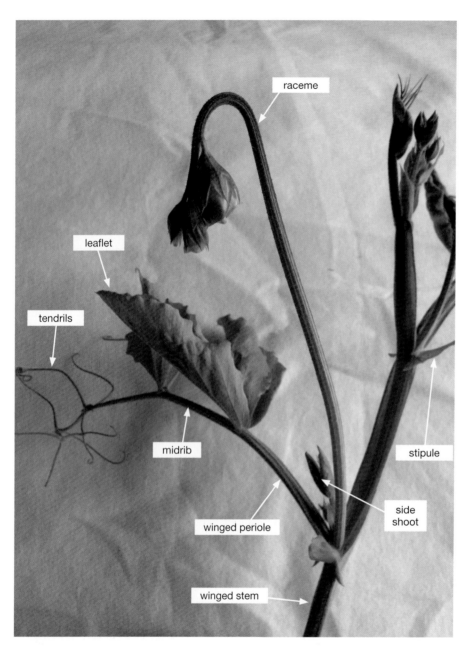

Vegetative parts of the Sweet Pea.

in shape; two horizontal petals known as wings (ala); and a pair of small petals fused together to form a keel (carina), named in allusion to its boat-like appearance. Some keels are open and some are clamped around the stamens and style (reproductive organs).

The reproductive parts consist of ten stamens and a style. Each stamen (androecium) consists of a pollen-bearing anther on the end of a filament. Nine of the filaments are fused together, leaving one free, but the anthers are all free and clustered around the style. The gynoecium consists of a stigma on the end of a style. The style is flattened, with a brush of hairs on the inner face, and twisted anti-clockwise through 90°. Following pollination, a legume forms. This is linear in shape, consisting

Parts of the raceme.

carina (keel)

vexillum (standard or banner)

ala (wings)

calyx

pedicel

peduncle

of two valves that are usually hairy on the outside and without wings. Seeds are attached to the inside of the legume wall by a slither of plant tissue called a funiculus. Each seed has a smooth seed coat which is interrupted by a short line known as the hilum. Seeds are dehiscent, i.e. they are dispersed by the valves springing open and scattering the seeds.

GROWTH CYCLE

As with all annuals, the life cycle begins and ends with a seed. Seeds can remain dormant for several years, awaiting the right conditions for their growth cycle to begin. Germination is initiated by moisture and temperature. In its native Sicily, rainfall is normally light during the summer months of June to

August. The cycle begins with early autumn rains, while temperatures are still warm, and finishes as the seeds ripen in the summer sun.

Seed germination

Water is absorbed by the seed which then swells and sends out a primary root, or radical, through the hilum. In order for the germinating seed to thrive, the root needs anchorage, water, air and nutrients. Anchorage is provided in nature by soil but may be provided by gardeners through another growing medium. The medium needs to have a balance between water and air. Too much water will fill the pores in the soil or medium so that air is excluded. The root becomes waterlogged and

Germinating seed, showing the primary root and shoot emerging from the hilum.

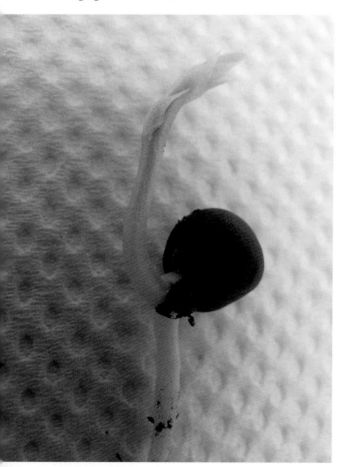

will drown. Too little water and the root will dry out. Root initiation is followed by the emergence from the seed of a primary shoot, or hypocotyl, which has two cotyledon leaves on opposite sides of the shoot.

The initial growth has been sustained by nutrients within the seed but must be continued by the plant having access to sunlight and to nutrients in the soil. Sunlight enables the plant's green tissues to photosynthesize, which is the process by which the energy of the sunlight is used to build up complex substances from carbon dioxide and water. Nutrients are absorbed as solutions by osmosis through the root, which continues to elongate and to branch out. As the root system develops, it forms an association with specific bacteria so that nodules start to appear on the roots. This characteristic is common to leguminous plants, such as peas and beans, and allows the plants to 'fix' their own nitrogen from the air within the soil. The roots will also form an association with specific mycorrhizal fungi, if present, which enhances the ability of the roots to absorb nutrients. The extent to which the root system develops will depend on how windy the site is and on the availability of water and nutrients. Plants grown in a freely draining medium within the shelter of a glasshouse, which are receiving frequent applications of water and nutrients, have no need to develop an extensive root system so instead they develop a tiny root system.

Primary shoot development

As a result of these inputs, which fuel cell division within the plant, the young plant is slowly able to develop. The primary shoot extends in length and the first pair of true leaves is formed. All green plant tissue has the capacity to photosynthesize but the true leaves are the real drivers of this process. Growth continues by the extension of internodal stem leading to the creation of each node. Internodes (the distance between nodes) are quite short at this stage but will elongate as the plant builds up strength. The rate of growth should now start to increase until cold winter temperatures encourage the development of side growths at the base of the primary shoot. As internodes develop,

Plants will naturally produce side shoots so these must be removed when growing cordon plants.

In nature, the plant will complete its life cycle where it started but the gardener can manipulate the location for their own needs. Plants can be moved at any stage in their early growth cycle but the younger they are, the easier it is to move them. Once the growth surge associated with spring begins, root damage is inevitable so that a check to growth occurs and they never seem to recover as well. The clever gardener produces plants in a way that prevents such a check to growth occurring.

DETERMINATE VERSUS INDETERMINATE GROWTH

Primary shoot growth is generally determinate and leads to the production of indeterminate side shoots. The growth we see in most Sweet Peas is indeterminate, by which we mean the shoots will continue to elongate and form leaves until the plant sets seed to complete its cycle. Dwarf Sweet Peas are indeterminate but have very short internodes so that the length of stem remains short. Some intermediate height varieties are determinate, though some of these are indeterminate with longer internodes than dwarf types.

Vegetative growth

Leaves on the young plant consist of a single pair of leaflets but as the plant develops tendrils start to form. Initially these are a single tendril that appears as an extension of the midrib from between the pair of leaflets. As more growth occurs, branched tendrils appear, except in non-tendril varieties where the more primitive leaf form, with extra pairs of leaflets, occurs. The indeterminate growth means that the plant haulm will trail along the ground unless it has some form of support to enable it to climb. Gardeners will

they start to form wings of flat tissue on opposite sides. Stipules also form at the nodes and like the wings they have some capacity to photosynthesize. All vegetative parts are small at this stage but the increase in capacity to photosynthesize has a snow-balling effect so that the parts increase in size as the plant continues to grow. During late winter, the side shoots will develop at a greater rate than the original primary shoot to an extent that the latter normally fizzles out in the spring.

provide this artificially but in nature the plant uses its tendrils to cling to other plants and secure upright growth. In time, more side shoots start to develop along the side shoots, known as tertiary growths because they occur on secondary growths. Younger leaves are more photosynthetically active so, as growth progresses, new leaves are formed and the older ones are jettisoned. This is achieved by transporting plant compounds from the older leaves to areas of active growth. The older leaves then turn yellow, and eventually brown, as their usefulness to the plant decreases.

Flower initiation

The exact factors controlling flower initiation are not fully known but a combination of plant development, temperature and day length will lead the plant to form racemes, sometimes referred to as flower stems or flower spikes. The opening of the flower occurs in sequence, with the lowest flower opening first and the uppermost flower opening last. Flowers are placed alternately along one side of the raceme so that there is a front and a back to the whole raceme. The lowest flower faces left or right, when looking at the front of the raceme, the direction apparently being randomly chosen.

The speed with which a flower opens varies with temperature and day length. On warm summer days, a guide from when the buds are first seen until full flowering is two weeks. Petals unfurl quickly and correctly in these conditions. On colder days, unfurling is slower and there is more risk of malformation occurring. Malformation is discussed later in this chapter. Very hot conditions can encourage flowers to open too quickly, bringing further problems of bloom formation. Availability to the plant of potassium and of water encourages flowers to open cleanly.

Setting seed

The first flowers produced by a plant may be underdeveloped but on the whole the first real flush of blooms has the longest racemes but is unlikely to set seed. As the flowering season progresses, raceme length shortens and the likelihood of seeds forming increases. Flowering is a necessary prelude to setting seed. The plant is programmed to produce seed so if dead flower heads are removed, or if blooms are cut for decoration, it encourages the plant to produce more flowers. Seed set is more likely to occur during hot weather when the plant's entire metabolism is operating more quickly. Pollination occurs when the petals are still furled and before the flower opens. This self-pollination enables varieties to come true from seed. By the time the flower is fully open, self-pollination has occurred and the chances of cross-pollination by insects taking place are minimal. Cross-pollination cannot be entirely ruled out though, so that in any seed crop there is always the risk of a tiny percentage of rogues appearing in the next generation.

Racemes are formed in the leaf axils.

Young legume with seeds starting to form (K. Hammett).

The fact that the flowers do not need to open for pollination to occur may be the reason that the period of flowering for each raceme is so short. This aspect of evolution is more efficiently seen in the related species *Lathyrus gloeospermus* which is cleistogamous. This term is used to describe species that form seeds without the flowers fully developing. *L. gloeospermus* shows a tiny bud of tissue in the leaf axil that does not develop into a raceme and it only becomes apparent that the plant has 'flowered' and self-pollinated when the legume starts to appear. People often consider that cross-pollination occurs in Sweet Peas or else it would not need to produce scent. Surely the scent must be needed to attract insect pollinators? In my view, the scent in Sweet Peas is a redundant quality, rather like the appendix in humans, which had not been lost in the evolution of the wild species from cross-pollinating to self-pollinating. Some people would argue that the existence of scent in the Sweet Pea has been an extremely successful evolutionary asset that has enabled the species to be spread by humans throughout much of the world!

Upon flowering, the petals soon fade and fall, leaving the legume to develop. The lifeline for the seeds developing inside the legume is the funiculus. Sometimes problems can occur that inhibit seed formation but if all goes well the seeds will develop all that they need for the next generation of growth. Upon maturity, the seeds ripen, the funiculus dries and withers to a slither of dead tissue. The valves of the legume also dry out in warm, dry conditions and when fully dry, the two valves of the legume separate violently and twist open to fling the seeds to begin the next generation.

TIMING GROWTH FOR AN EVENT

Mention has already been made that it takes about two weeks during summer growing conditions from bloom initiation to full flowering. This quality can be manipulated by the gardener to maximize the chance of having as many blooms as possible on a certain day. This might be required when growing Sweet Peas to cut for a special occasion, such as a family wedding or for a flower show on a particular date. This is not an exact science: in very hot periods, flower development will take less than two weeks; in cold wet periods it will take longer. We cannot know at the start of the two weeks what the weather will do during that period.

Ages of raceme from the bottom: (1) older bloom with fading colour; (2) perfect bloom; (3) top flower still in bud; (4) bottom flower showing colour; (5) immature racemes.

However, good weather at the start of the period is a useful indicator that good quality blooms can be expected; poor weather at the start means that flowers may fail to develop properly and 'bud-drop', discussed in Chapter 8, may be expected. It is a useful guide for flower show managers on what sort of entry to expect in Sweet Pea classes.

One successful approach is to review how the racemes are developing four or five days before an event. Under normal conditions, one flower can be expected to open each day. It is therefore possible to see at this stage which raceme on a plant may be expected to be at full-flowering for the event, bearing in mind that cutting of blooms may be required on the day before the event. Now some racemes may appear to be developing quite normally to be at their best when required, but some may be a little behind and some a little advanced. The rate of development can now be slowed or quickened on those plants requiring it. The experienced grower will not have been too vigilant in removing side shoots or dead flowers. Removal of older racemes below the chosen one will slow down the development of the chosen raceme. Similarly, leaving the dead ones on the plant for a few days will help speed up the growth of the chosen raceme. A similar effect can be achieved with side shoots. Leaving side shoots on the plant will speed up development of the raceme while vigilantly removing them will slow it down. Plants should be checked daily during this period in order to make adjustments in the light of growth during the past twenty-four hours and prevailing weather conditions.

MALFORMATION

Typical Sweet Pea flowers have petals consisting of a standard, two wings and a keel. The nature of these varies with the type of Sweet Pea but there is also an issue that sometimes things go wrong during the development of a flower so that more petals appear, or petals become malformed in some way. The position of petals within the flower and the mechanisms that lead to malformation have been studied and described by Sydney Harrod.

Flower shapes

In its perfect form, the standard petal will be upright and flat: plain in the Grandiflora type while frilled, fluted or waved in the Spencer type. In reality, we regularly see departures from this ideal. Some standards may be hooded, in which the edge of the petal folds forward. This is inherent in some old-fashioned varieties. Some standards may be reflexed, presenting a concave face because the sides face backwards. This is sometimes associated with hot weather conditions. A stunted standard occurs when the top of the petal has not fully developed and this is associated with cold weather conditions. Another fault arises when standard petals are broad at the base so that this remains tucked into the calyx as the petal expands to form a bonnet shape. This too is associated with cold weather conditions. As with a stunted standard, some varieties are more prone than others. Applying potassium fertilizer helps reduce such problems by encouraging flower buds to open more quickly and correctly. Another fault arising from the opening of the bud is the formation of notches in the outline of the standard. These are usually seen as a pair of notches on opposite sides of the standard and are common in some old-fashioned varieties, e.g. 'America'.

Wings should normally be flat and spreading, almost in a horizontal plane, with an angle between the wings of 150° to 180°. In the Spencer form they should be wavy. An angle significantly less than 150° should be considered less than perfect, while drooping wings are definitely unattractive. The angle between the wings will in any event reduce during aging of the flower. The wings should also be symmetrical in their angle to the vertical, for example having one wing held horizontally while the other has dropped would give an asymmetric appearance.

Some wings may be furled rather than flat, i.e. the edge of the petal folds upwards, and this is considered exceptionally attractive by many as long as both wings are furled symmetrically. Conversely, wings where the edge of the petals is rolled downwards are considered faulty. Other patterns frequently encountered are pointed wings, when the petal has an angle in it, and aerofoil wings, when

An F2 bloom showing wings attractively furled but spoiled by a reflexed standard.

they are concave rather than flat. Stunted wings sometimes occur, usually to just one wing, when the wing is small and underdeveloped.

Keels are generally shielded from view by the wings but sometimes these split into their two components.

Deformities

Many of the 'faults' seen in Sweet Peas arise quite early through cell differentiation during formation of the flower bud. These are commonly known as malformation and include various outcomes, some of which are more attractive than others. The creation of extra petals, for example, provides a more frilly appearance to the flower which many find attractive and have led breeders to develop duplex varieties. Strictly speaking, a duplex flower is one with an additional standard petal but with no parts of any petal trapped into the calyx or other petals. In practice, duplex varieties have all sorts of other 'faults' that add to the general frilliness.

Faults that arise during bud formation include oversized standard or wing petals that are intermediate towards the formation of a second standard or wing. Where additional petals or extra-large petals arise, the developing bud is usually over-crowded so that the flower does not open cleanly but bits of petal remain trapped in the calyx or are out of sequence with adjacent petals.

Having said all the above, most people get enormous pleasure from their Sweet Peas without any concern for the occasional faulty flower that arises. Only in the wild Sweet Pea and some few varieties is malformation never seen. Malformation is only a problem for the flower show exhibitor.

Sweet Pea 'Angela Ann' showing malformation.

CHAPTER 4

Growing your own Sweet Peas

As with all species, having a good understanding of how the plants grow and develop in nature makes it much easier to understand the plant's needs and ensure success in your cultivation of Sweet Peas. This chapter transforms the principles outlined in the previous chapter into practical advice for gardeners of all levels of experience. In truth, Sweet Peas are one of the easiest plants to grow but the following is intended to help the reader enjoy better success, whatever the site and situation. Sweet Peas propagate very readily from seed but increasing in the western world is a trend for people to buy young plants.

PURCHASING PLANTS

There are three options in the UK for buying plants. The most commonly available, and perhaps the least desirable, is to buy plants from your local garden centre. In my experience, these vary in quality from the awful to the acceptable. At worst, garden centres are selling ten or more seedlings in a 3in (75mm) half pot. The period from sowing to sale may be as little as twenty-one days, as the plants have been forced to give soft elongated growth. They have no root system and they might be suitable for pricking out and growing on if not for the top growth being too elongated. They are sold as finished plants and planted out by hapless customers who later conclude, incorrectly, that they cannot grow Sweet Peas. The situation is now improving thanks to one very large nursery that is putting much more time and care into producing plants specifically for the garden centre and mail

Sweet Pea 'Anniversary' (S. Cuttle).

Seedsmen now offer an increasingly wide range of colours. This is Sweet Pea 'Geoff Hughes'.

order markets. Some exceptional garden centres may be selling good quality plants, locally sourced. Treasure it if your local garden centre is one of these.

The second option is to buy plants by mail order, through a catalogue or via the internet. These usually come as plugs and should arrive as good quality young plants. Try ordering autumn-sown plants where the option is available, but these tend to be mixtures rather than individual varieties. Spring-sown plants are more commonly available, which can mean they were sown any time after the beginning of January. It is now possible to buy these in a reasonable range of individual named varieties as well as mixtures. Early ordering is recommended.

The third option is to buy your plants from a Sweet Pea specialist. This may be an amateur enthusiast living in your locality or one of the specialist seedsmen and plant producers. Plants are normally only available for collection though it is worth asking if they are willing to mail them. Placing an order in late summer or early autumn enables the grower to provide the exact varieties that you want at the time that you want them. These plants will be grown to the same standard as the grower's own plants and will have had a long growing period to develop strength.

PURCHASING SEEDS

It really is very easy to produce excellent quality plants from your own sowing. This is also the most economical way to get your plants and is less work than some people may suppose. There is also something very satisfying about nurturing your own plants from sowing to flowering. Garden centres normally stock Sweet Pea seeds from one or two generalist seed merchants. Some of these show more interest in Sweet Peas than others and the quality varies from one seed merchant to another. The term 'seed merchant' is used because they have usually bought the seed from a wholesale supplier rather than had it grown specifically for them.

Mail order or internet purchasing gives a much wider range of suppliers and a complete range of varieties. As well as the generalist seed merchants, there are businesses in the UK and USA, and elsewhere, that specialize in Sweet Peas. Most will have seed grown especially for them under contract, giving them a direct relationship with the seed producer. The best produce their own

Commercial trade stand at an RHS Flower Show (C. Ball).

seed, giving them direct control over production to ensure that seed is saved only from the best plants. The worst have simply bought their seed from wholesale suppliers.

Having a choice of varieties is important to ensure that you get the ones most suited to your needs. It should be clear from the above that the quality of the stock of a popular variety, offered by many seedsmen, may be variable. Learning by trial and error is the best way so start by getting a little seed from many suppliers and you will soon learn which supply seed that germinates very well and produces flowers that live up to expectations. As a short cut, try to avoid cheap packets of seed. Once purchased, your seed should remain viable for at least two years so it is a good idea to initially get twice as much as you need. This avoids the potential frustration, if needing to re-sow because of losses, of going back to your seedsman for more seed, only to find that they have sold out of the variety you are growing. UK-grown seed is most plentiful in the autumn after harvest so experienced growers will purchase then, even if not sowing until spring, in order to ensure the varieties they want are available.

SOWING SEEDS

What is in the packet?

On opening your seed packets, the first thing that becomes evident is that varieties vary enormously in the size of seeds, their colour and whether they are round or wrinkled in shape. Colours vary between pale brown, deep brown, black, grey and mottled. There is no doubt that having large, round, plump seeds, so called 'bold' seeds, look the most impressive but the simple fact is that some really excellent varieties always produce small wrinkled seeds, e.g. 'Lake Windermere'. Size is therefore not a guide to the eventual performance of the variety. Size affects the amount of food stored in the seed for growth during germination, but following germination photosynthesis takes over and all plants that have germinated start on an equal basis. Variations in the vigour of varieties at this stage are due to genetic factors rather than seed size.

SELECTING SEEDS FROM THE PACKET

If sowing a mixture, it is important not to discard any seeds that are small and wrinkled since you will simply be reducing the number of varieties from your mixture. On the other hand, when sowing an individual variety, an odd seed that is the wrong shape, size or colour may be an indication that it is not the correct variety. Such odd ones should either be discarded or sown and marked separately. Any seeds that have a split seed coat are at higher risk of damping off. Some varieties are more prone than others to producing split seeds. A reputable seedsman will have discarded these but the odd one may have slipped through into the packet. You should also discard any that look a bit mouldy, though again these will normally have been discarded prior to packeting.

Some seeds may still have the funiculus attached at one end of the hilum. This makes no difference to germination but some people incorrectly think it is a shrivelled radical and that the seed has started to germinate in the packet! Most seedsmen add an extra seed or two to the number stated on the packet. I once had a customer tell me that his germination had been 'better than 100 per cent'. When I challenged this, he said that the number bought had all germinated plus the extra one or two in each packet!

In deciding how many seeds to sow, a starting point should be the number of plants that you want to end up with. Germination should be 90 per cent or more from a good seed source but allow 80 per cent if you are unsure of your supplier. Allow that a few plants may fail prior to planting out. So if your aim is to have fifty plants for planting out, you should at least sow between sixty and seventy seeds. Some people like to sow more since this allows them to eventually plant only the strongest plants and it allows more of a buffer for unexpected losses. Any spare plants that are eventually not needed will always be found a welcome home among friends and relatives.

Dates for sowing

When to sow depends very much on your location and when flowers are required. Conditions will vary with local microclimates but, as a guide for outdoor growing, Sweet Pea enthusiasts in the southern half of the UK sow in October while those in the northern half sow in January to mid February. Later chapters deal with conditions in other countries and cultivation under glass or polythene, where sowing times may vary. Top quality plants can easily be achieved by sowing at any time between October and mid-February. Earlier than this, say September, leads to excess soft shoot growth that can then be cut down by frost when winter sets in. October has the benefit that ambient temperatures are still sufficiently mild for outdoor germination. By November, temperatures have normally fallen so that a little night-time warmth is required to aid germination. On the south coast of England, the optimum time for sowing is late October but earlier is better further north; say the second week in October in the north midlands.

Spring sowing, generally January but mid-February in Scotland, is preferred further north because winter light levels are poor and the plants may not thrive from an autumn sowing. In addition, conditions for planting out may not arise until later. This timescale still allows for the production of top quality blooms. It is the amateur gardener sowing in March and April who misses the opportunity for the plants to build strength during a longer growth period before they start to think about flowering.

Pre-germination treatment of seeds

Much advice on sowing Sweet Pea seed states that you should chip the seed, i.e. break the seed coat on the side away from the hilum, using a razor blade or gently rubbing with sandpaper. Other advice is that this should not be done. This creates a very confusing situation for the beginner, so which is right? The surprising answer is that both may be correct. When a seed supplier tells you that you should or should not chip, their advice is best heeded. The reason for this is that the seedsman knows where the seed was produced and whether or not it has too hard a seed coat. The confusion

If chipping seeds prior to germination, be sure to avoid cutting the hilum.

Seeds on right swollen after soaking. The straight line on each seed is the hilum.

arises because at one time most of the Sweet Pea seed sold in the UK was produced in California and developed an unnaturally hard seed coat. The seed would not germinate well unless the hard seed coat was broken. Nowadays, more seed is produced in a temperate climate, such as New Zealand and the UK, where the seed coat is not too hard. Some gardeners still prefer to chip their seed even when this is not necessary. Apart from being an unnecessary and tedious job (can you imagine me doing this with 4,000 seeds?), there is a risk of the same problems that arise with soaking seeds.

Rather than chip their Sweet Pea seeds, some gardeners like to soak them in water overnight prior to sowing. Any that do not swell are then mechanically chipped. Research published in the 1990s showed that soaking seeds that were produced in a temperate climate can in fact reduce germination for those varieties that are naturally softer seeded.

Method of sowing

Every Sweet Pea specialist has their own preferred way of sowing seeds, achieved through trial and error. The traditional commercial method was to sow eight seeds in a 5in (125mm) flower pot, reducing the number of plants to six if necessary following germination. This size of pot gives a good depth for root growth and represents efficient use of growing medium and space but has the disadvantage that some root damage is inevitable if separating the plants for planting out individually. This is still a good method if growing as a clump so that the plants do not require separation. Where the plants are to be planted individually, some form of cellular system is preferred so that there is no root damage to cause a check in growth following planting. Options include Rootrainers, 3½in (90mm) flower pots, coffee cups with holes punched in the bottoms, rolled newspaper, and toilet roll centres, among others.

Much preferred are 5in (125mm) deep Rootrainers, known as Sherwoods, and made from recycled plastic. As I sow 4,000 seeds each year, I would struggle to produce enough toilet roll centres for these! The Sherwoods provide thirty-two cells in the area of a standard seed tray and have a number of advantages over other cellular systems. They consist of a holder into which are placed eight plastic 'books'. Each book folds together to form four cells and they sit in the holder so that an air gap exists between the base of each book and the

Pre-germination of seeds on moist paper prior to space sowing.

work surface. The inside of each cell is ridged so that roots are channelled downwards. When the roots reach the space at the bottom, instead of circling the base they are 'air pruned', which encourages the roots to make new side growth rather than elongate further. At planting time, each book is opened to reveal four plants that are quickly and easily planted. The cells can be re-used and last for years. A few growers prefer the larger Jumbo rootrainers that have an 8in (200mm) depth but this is wasteful of growing medium.

Choice of growing medium

The term 'growing medium' has become established in the UK as a definitive term for what many people still call 'compost'. In this book, the term compost is reserved for waste organic material that has gone through a composting process.

As with containers, growing medium is a matter of personal preference but my recommendation is to use a moss peat multipurpose product with added John Innes fertilizer. I have never got on with John Innes soil-based growing media, finding them too finely milled. A similar problem occurs with sedge peat growing media. These may be all right for bedding plants and other spring-sown plants, which are in them for a relatively short period, but for autumn sowing you need a coarser growing medium that still provides air to the roots after the winter rains have compacted it. Sieving the growing medium will reduce the coarseness and is not necessary for such a large seed as a Sweet Pea. Some growers like to add fine grit, perlite or vermiculite in order to introduce coarseness into a compost. If you must use John Innes, then No. 1 provides the optimum level of nutrients. There are all sorts of peat alternatives but nothing quite beats a moss peat growing medium; in a 90:10 ratio with sand.

USE OF PEAT ALTERNATIVES

The problem with existing non-peat alternatives such as coir and those based on composted bark or other material is that they do not retain nutrients so that frequent winter feeding is required in order to produce half-decent plants. One environmental gain is therefore counteracted by the other. It is also more difficult to manage the water content of the non-peat growing medium. Most dry quickly on the surface but retain moisture below making it easy to over-water plants. With further research, it is to be hoped that an alternative to peat suitable for Sweet Peas will soon arise before all of the world's peat bogs are destroyed!

Having chosen your container, fill this with growing medium to the top and then gently tap the container, whatever sort, on a hard surface so that the growing medium settles into any air pockets. In some cases, it may then be necessary to top up the growing medium so that it is no more than 10mm (½in) from the top. This allows the full depth of the container to be available for root development. The seeds are large enough to be individually spaced on the surface of the growing medium. Germination should be so good that one seed per cell is enough but, in order to have no empty cells, some may prefer to sow two seeds per cell and then remove the weaker if both germinate. Prior to sowing, it is very beneficial to treat each seed batch with a pinch of seed dressing, according to availability. This is a powder fungicide that prevents 'damping off' disease and is more effective than watering the growing medium with a liquid fungicide after sowing.

Sowing depth

It has been suggested that some Sweet Pea colours are quicker to germinate than others but this has not been my experience. Some colours are associated with particular seed sizes or hardness of seed

coat but these are an unintended result of seedling selection by hybridizers rather than a genetic link with flower colour. Hardness of seed coat affects how quickly moisture is absorbed. Seed size will have an impact if seeds are sown at the same depth since the amount of growing medium covering them will be less with a larger seed. They would then reach the surface more quickly than a smaller seed sown at the same depth.

Once the seed is sown, it should be lightly covered with growing medium so that it is about 5mm (¼in) below the surface. You will find some general garden writers recommending that Sweet Pea seeds should be sown 60mm (2in) deep, presumably copying the wisdom of some other garden writer who, like themselves, has never actually grown Sweet Peas. Better to have only the shallowest of covering so the hypocotyl gets to the light earlier.

Some growers like to pre-germinate their seeds by placing them in a warm place between sheets of wet, moisture-absorbent paper. After a few days, the radical starts to emerge and they then space sow only those seeds that have started to germinate. This ensures there will be no empty cells but is quite a lot of additional work that is unnecessary. It is more efficient to minimize the number of operations and handling.

Emerging shoot.

After sowing

Apart from lightly tapping the container to settle the growing medium prior to sowing, at no other time should this be compacted, either before or after sowing. Once sown, the seeds should be gently watered using a watering can with a fine rose and this provides all the compaction that is needed. Any additional firming of the growing medium will merely reduce the amount of air within it, thus removing one of the essential factors that enable the seed to grow and develop. Growing medium should be kept on the dry side following this initial watering to avoid the risk of 'damping off'. Some growers cover their containers with dry newspaper following sowing, apparently to help avoid crusting of the surface. Such crusting should not occur if a suitable growing medium is used and compaction avoided, so the practice is superfluous. It also runs the risk of emerging plants becoming drawn if the grower is insufficiently vigilant in removing the paper as soon as they start to emerge.

Germination generally takes around two weeks but only one week if germinated in warm conditions. They can be germinated without heat during the winter but it may take up to a month and there is an increased risk that during this time the seed rots in the cold dampness of the growing medium.

CARE OF YOUNG PLANTS

The first months of the young plant's life in many ways are more important than the months after planting out. If you have a good plant by the spring, you can ruin it after planting but if you have a poor plant by the spring, nothing you will do can turn this into a good plant. Some people like to apply biostimulants or beneficial fungi at this stage but they are discussed later as they are more relevant to plants following spring planting.

Protection of plants

Depending on your circumstances, it may be necessary to protect seeds against mice and slugs. Mice in particular can destroy an entire batch of emerging or young germinated plants by eating the swollen remains of the seed at the base of the plant. Guidance on protection against mice is given in Chapter 8.

If germinated using heat, plants should be removed from heat at this stage or they become elongated.

Mouse-resistant benching. The canes supporting wire to keep off birds should be further apart to be fully mouse-proof.

People sometimes experience failure from an autumn sowing because they mollycoddle their plants too much. An October sowing will germinate outside but some prefer to place them in a cold glasshouse or cold frame. Once the seedlings emerge, it pays to grow them as hard as you dare and your microclimate allows. If sowing with night-time heat during the winter, containers should be moved to a cold frame or cold glasshouse as soon as the plants begin to emerge through the growing medium. Any delay runs the risk that the plants will become elongated. Sweet Peas will not only happily tolerate frost down to –5°C (23°F) unprotected, they will benefit from it once the leaves have developed. The root ball may be frozen solid for several days but no problems should arise, especially if slow thawing occurs. Anything colder than this, some protection is

advisable, such as a cold frame or cold glasshouse, but no heat. Long periods of severe weather may see plants happily tucked under a covering of old blankets or fleece with no access to daylight but on mild, sunny, winter days, having the plants outside is essential to their wellbeing. Although plants are frost-tolerant, protection against very strong winds is very important since these can cause physical damage, especially icy, winter winds. The enthusiast is ever-vigilant to the changing weather.

Should plants be 'stopped'?

As with chipping, another aspect of growing Sweet Peas where conflicting advice confuses the novice is when, and if, to remove the growing point, sometimes known as 'pinching out' or 'stopping'. October-sown plants grown cold will have reached

Young plants showing side shoots starting to emerge.

75mm (3in) high by the middle of January and side shoots will start to form naturally at that time. It is a grave mistake to stop such plants as this encourages the growth of side shoots at a time when such growth is not wanted. Many a grower has stopped plants and then finds in a mild winter that they are ready for planting out by the end of January but ground and weather conditions are unsuitable. Left unstopped, those side shoots that are starting to form in January will be just the right length for planting out in March. It is the cold weather that encourages natural side shoot development. By the beginning of February, if side shoots have not started to form it is a sure sign that you have not been growing your plants hard enough. At this time, just look over each plant as there may be an odd one that refuses to produce any side shoots and these can then be safely stopped. Of course, plants that are sown late or are grown in a heated glasshouse for early cut flowers will not experience a cold spell and these should be pinched once at least four true leaves have developed.

It is possible to propagate Sweet Peas from cuttings. This may seem more trouble than it is worth when they grow so readily from seeds, but the technique can prove useful if dealing with one, or just a few, plant(s) that are particularly prized, for example in a breeding programme. It enables the grower to double the number of plants of a variety by allowing the young plant to grow on and then taking a soft tip cutting as a way of stopping the plant. The cutting needs to be inserted in an open

Traditional trench digging.

growing medium with bottom heat at around 15°C (60°F), where it should root quite readily. Plants are then grown as if propagated by seed.

GROUND PREPARATION

While your plants are slowly developing over the winter, this is the time to be preparing the ground where they will be planted. This is a difficult aspect on which to generalize since everyone's ground is different and a good grower has learnt what suits his own garden or plot best of all. Some like to prepare their ground even before they sow their seeds, because it is wet land for winter cultivation or because they want to allow as long a period as possible for winter weathering and for rainfall penetration of the broken ground. At the other extreme, some growing on a shallow, freely draining soil such as chalk prefer to leave

their ground preparation until the end of the winter since any goodness they incorporate from manures or fertilizer is quickly leached out of the topsoil by winter rains. As a general rule, it is best to finish preparing the ground before the New Year begins since this is the milder part of the winter when it is more pleasant to work and the soil has been set up for weathering by frost and rain. It is also better that the ground has time to settle prior to planting.

Depth of cultivation

Old gardening books claimed that ground for Sweet Peas should be cultivated to a depth of several feet and went into elaborate detail explaining how to double dig a plot by trenching. Copious quantities of manure or garden compost were incorporated into both subsoil and topsoil during this process. Nowadays, this is rarely considered necessary. Those growing on shallow soil above chalk need to do all they can to increase the depth of topsoil and to improve its moisture retaining capacity and humus level. Those growing on light, sandy soil also need to incorporate plenty of manure or garden compost. But for most gardeners, digging down to 45cm (18in) in the first year in order to break up the subsoil and then, in later years, simply working the topsoil is sufficient. Those with heavy clay subsoil may need to work this for more than one year but they will be well rewarded by having a wonderful, friable, mineral-rich soil. There will be those who argue that no cultivation is even better, relying on mulches to incorporate humus, and this may be appropriate on some sites. However, cultivating ensures that any perennial weeds are removed if, like me, you are not always sufficiently vigilant to ensure they do not arise in the first place!

Enriching the soil

There is no doubt that incorporating manure or garden compost may be beneficial but it can be overdone. Some problems can arise if too much manure is given, or it is too fresh, as we shall see in the chapter on keeping plants healthy. Those on a hungry soil, such as chalk or sand, need to apply plenty, as long as it is well-rotted. Where soil has been long cultivated, or is naturally very fertile, it may be best practice to incorporate manure every second year instead of yearly. The same can be said about incorporating artificial fertilizers. A hungry soil will mean that your plants need a base fertilizer incorporated prior to planting, plus subsequent feeding once the plants are in the ground. Popular choices with UK gardeners include blood, fish and bone; Vitax Q4 or a slow-release granular fertilizer. For most gardeners, however, no fertilizer should be required. In fact, applying a nitrogen fertilizer will inhibit the plant's ability to fix its own nitrogen. The best approach to fertilizers is to have your topsoil tested during the winter period and incorporate only where a deficiency is indicated. My soil is naturally deficient in potassium so needs a top dressing of sulphate of potash prior to planting. Applying potassium may be beneficial for other locations since it helps the petals to open

more quickly and reduces the risk of malformation. It is also beneficial when growing to produce seeds, for example when raising new varieties. However, too much potassium can inhibit the plant's ability to take up other minerals, such as magnesium and manganese.

If breaking new ground prior to planting, incorporating the turf seems to be beneficial though the benefit is probably greater on hungry soils. If they are available, old turves can be incorporated into the ground in any year to achieve a similar benefit. For those growing Sweet Peas on the same ground each year, green manures are becoming increasingly popular in the UK, particularly Caliente Mustard, which is claimed to act as a bio-fumigant. This may be beneficial when the plants are removed early but my own cropping does not allow sufficient time to have tried it.

Another benefit of soil testing is that it gives a measure of calcium, usually applied as garden lime. The aim should be to have a pH of between 6.0 and 6.5. Anything less than this means there is insufficient calcium available to ensure the supply of nitrogen to the plant. Anything more than 6.5 increases the risk that calcium will inhibit the uptake of other minerals.

USE OF BONEMEAL FERTILIZER

Many gardeners like to apply bonemeal prior to planting in order to supply phosphate to encourage early root development. This is a complete waste of time since the bonemeal breaks down too slowly to have any beneficial effect on the plants and there will already be sufficient phosphate in the soil, unless a deficiency has been indicated. The only purpose in recommending that gardeners should apply bonemeal is if they feel a need to apply something – it won't do any good but they can do no harm with it. And besides, how else would we dispose of dead animals?

Young plants grown in Sherwood Rootrainers and ready for planting out.

PLANTING IN FLOWERING POSITIONS

As soon as the side growths are large enough and soil conditions allow, the young plants should be planted into their flowering positions. This will be March in southern England, even late February is not unknown on the south coast. It may not be until May in colder parts of Scotland. Although there may be frosts and icy winds after such a planting date, the worst of these should have passed. In an exposed position it would be helpful to provide the plants with some shelter from north and east winds by providing a temporary windbreak made by stretching polythene or other material between stakes. In the worst situation, leaflets may turn yellow and the plant appears to be lost, but a hard-grown plant, or a spring-sown plant well weaned to the cold, will shoot again from the base and still gains overall benefit from early planting. Now the roots can really expand to enable months of vigorous growth before daylight is sufficiently long for the plant to turn to flower initiation. Those growing in containers may be able to locate these somewhere sheltered, but unheated, with a view to moving the container to its flowering position at a later date.

Preparing soil tilth

The ground where your Sweet Peas are to be planted should be raked to break up any clods and provide a fine, even surface into which plants can be inserted. Planting is much like any other soft-tissued plant, such as a bedding plant. A trowel is preferred to a dibber since a dibber tends to compact the soil around the sides of the hole it makes. Loose soil is better, which is then gently compacted by hand after the plant is inserted. The depth of planting should be sufficient to just cover the root ball so that the top of the root ball is at or a fraction below the soil surface. In some years, a very wet spring may mean that plants could spoil if left in their winter container too long, waiting for the right conditions. One way to overcome this is to cover the ground with a sheet of polythene, tarpaulin, or similar for a few weeks prior to planting so that the planting surface is not sodden. Another is to backfill around the rootball with a multipurpose growing medium rather than wet soil that cannot be firmed around the rootball. Whether wet or dry, plants should always be watered immediately after planting to allow the soil to settle into any air pockets.

If you have produced your young plants in some form of biodegradable container, such as a peat pot, roll of newspaper or toilet roll centre, it is essential to remove or break up the container prior to planting. This is because the container will not degrade quickly enough to allow the young roots to penetrate so that growth of the plant will be inhibited. It may be necessary at this stage to protect your plants against slugs, depending on your situation.

Giving the plants a good start is essential and various aids have become available in recent years. Most popular are the growth stimulants that use various forms of plant extract to stimulate plant growth. These have various modes of action but all work on the principle of stimulating growth to enable plants to better fend off fungal and bacterial attack. Some are claimed to include properties that are antifungal and/or antibacterial and they may have some benefit.

Beneficial fungi

Products that contain the fungus *Trichoderma harsianum* are more impressive. This is a benign fungus that wraps itself around the plant roots and out-competes parasitic fungi, preventing their ingress into plants via the root system. *Trichoderma* is not yet readily available and is horribly expensive but there are real benefits from using it on ground infected with verticillium. Mycorrhiza are more readily available but are not specific to Sweet Peas. Incorporating some topsoil, from where Sweet Peas have previously grown, into your growing medium may provide mycorrhiza, if present, but it will also provide weed seeds and risks introducing soil-borne pests. Sweet Pea enthusiasts tend to use the same ground for their plants each year and this should facilitate the accumulation of naturally occurring mycorrhiza and builds fertility in the soil. The downside is that it also facilitates the accumulation of soil-borne diseases. A five-year rotation may be the optimum.

Temporary wind-break protection after planting protects against cold north and east winds.

CHAPTER 5

Sweet Peas in the garden

Sweet Pea 'Chance'
(C. Ball).

Sweet Peas may be grown in the garden for decorative purposes or they may be considered as cut flower crop production. If grown for decorative purposes, their position will need to be considered within the overall layout of the garden. A sunny spot is preferred but not one that is too hot. In a hot climate, if possible choose a position where some natural shade arises from a tree or building during the hottest part of the day but otherwise they get plenty of sunlight. This also applies in more temperate climates during hot years but the problem is that we cannot predict what the season will be like. Similarly, growing against a wall is a blessing in a cold wet summer but ruins the plants in a hot year. You could spread the risk by having some in a variety of locations.

A young 'hedge' of Sweet Peas at Wisley Gardens, supported using woven birch twigs.

METHODS OF SUPPORT

Consideration needs to be given to how your plants will be supported. Dwarf varieties need no support and can be allowed to trail along the ground. Even these however can look particularly attractive if given a short cane, 45cm (18in) high, into which the branched haulm is tied in order to give an upright habit. It is the taller growing varieties where support is normally considered essential. These can be allowed to simply trail along the ground, sending up racemes from ground level, but there are few garden situations where this might be considered attractive. Better to provide some sort of support and the choice depends on whether plants are being grown naturally or as cordons. When grown naturally, the plant is allowed to produce side shoots at will and the only pruning needed is the removal of dying flowers to prolong the flowering period. The traditional method of producing cut flowers, for sale or exhibition, is to grow the plants as cordons. With cordon plants, only one side shoot is trained up the support while all other side growths are removed so that all the plant's energy is channelled into the one shoot to produce larger flowers on longer racemes.

The choice of supports for naturally grown plants is almost as wide as the imagination. Bird houses, shrubs and derelict sheds have all been used. For me, the most attractive support for garden decoration is to use traditional pea sticks made from the brushwood of hazel, birch, sweet chestnut, or whatever branched twigs are locally available. These are simply inserted into the ground around the plants, which can then scramble up through them. Also effective are columns or lines of netting made from wire or plastic. The wire or plastic mesh used must be very open, around 15cm (6in) between strands is the optimum. Closer meshes, such as chicken wire, do not allow easy passage on the plants through them so they may distort growth, and the wire is more visible. Some people like to grow sweet peas along a fence or wall but there is still a need for some form of support for the plants to cling onto.

The cordon system

If growing cordons, the traditional method is to plant in nursery rows, supporting the plants using bamboo canes or hazel rods, which should ideally be 2.4m (8ft) long. Cordon-grown plants quickly reach the top of the cane and need to be lowered so additional canes need to be placed at the end of a single row to allow for this. It is therefore more usual to plant in double rows to facilitate lowering, a process that will be explained shortly. You will need one cane or rod for each plant. Rather than tie opposite canes together at the top, try securing the tops of the canes to wires stretched between two posts at either end of the double row. This avoids the blooms getting spoiled by other plants when they reach the top of the canes. A small piece of wood is placed at the top of each post to make a 'T' shape and two wires are stretched along the length of the double row. The canes are inserted into the ground along the length of each

row and the tops tied to the wire above that row. Some people prefer to put one or more further rows of wire lower down the canes but these risk interfering with plant growth.

Maintenance of cordon plants

Extra tasks for the cordon grower include removing side shoots, removing tendrils and tying into the canes or other support. In the old days, plants were literally tied to the canes using raffia or garden twine, making this a long slow job that has to be repeated every time the plants are lowered. Nowadays, rings are most commonly used but some growers prefer a Max Tapener machine rather than rings. This secures the plant to the cane by stapling a plastic band to form a ring. These machines are very popular with some growers but take a bit of getting used to. They are

Tom Jones of Ruabon invented the cordon system around 1905 to 1910.

Lowering of cordon plants.

quick to use, once mastered, but the used tape needs to be removed at the end of the season.

Side shoots should not be removed religiously but always leave one or two in reserve near the growing point. Try allowing them to grow up to 2 inches during the flowering season as this gives flexibility depending on the prevailing weather conditions or when timing the production of blooms for an event. They also act as a reserve if the main growing point goes blind or is accidentally damaged. Removing tendrils has no impact on how well the plants grow. It is done to prevent the tendril hooking around the haulm or raceme of a neighbouring plant, which then distorts the growth and leads to bent racemes.

With all the plant's vigour channelled into a single cordon, plants may soon reach the top of their canes. This requires the plants to be lowered when they are about 1.8m (6ft) high. Each plant is untied from its cane and carefully laid along the row so that the top 60cm (2ft) can be bent upwards and tied to the bottom of a cane 1.2m

(4ft) from where the plant is growing. They are then able to grow to the tops of their new canes. This process can be repeated as often as necessary. By the end of the season, you may have a cordon 4.5m (15ft) long, growing up a cane a long distance from where it started. The benefit of having a double row is that when the plants reach the end of their row, they can be turned through 180° to travel in the opposite direction along the opposite row. Lowering takes a bit of courage the first time you do it but the resulting blooms make it all worthwhile.

SETTING OUT PLANTS

One aspect where views differ is whether you should put the supports in place first and then plant next to them; or plant out first and then place the supports next to the plants. Those who advocate planting out first will point to the need to get the plants into the ground as soon as conditions allow for planting, leaving time to place supports at leisure. Those who advocate supports first point to the risk of root damage when canes or rods are inserted next to the young plants. I use both methods depending on the means of support. When plants are being grown as cordons, the canes are set in position first and then one plant is placed at the base of each cane. When plants are being grown along rows of netting, these are planted in a line between the posts that will support the netting. The posts are a permanent feature and the netting does not go into the ground so there is no risk of root damage by this method.

Spacing between plants

Spacing between plants will depend on the method of growing. Naturally grown plants will give a very good effect if planted 15cm (6in) apart. Closer than this is fine, but unnecessary. Further apart, at say 30cm (1ft) spacing will also give a good effect but more sparse. How vigorously they will grow depends very much on the individual microclimate and on soil conditions, so there can be no hard and fast rule about spacing.

Distances for cordon plants are more clear cut. Within each row, plants should be around 190mm (7½in) apart. More than this will give the plants more light; less and they become too crowded. The distance between a pair of rows depends on the angle of the canes. If the rows are planted 30cm (12in) apart, the canes will be vertical. If space allows, some prefer to make the rows wider apart at the base, up to 45cm (18in), so that the rows of canes are leaning in to each other. A few growers prefer the two rows to be very close, 15cm (6in) apart, with canes leaning away from each other. The reason for an angle is to ensure the raceme

Uniform height along a line of cordon plants following lowering (A. Hubbuck).

remains as straight as possible along its full length, for exhibition purposes. Cut flower growers are content with vertical supports to get more plants into a given area. If growing more than one double row, paths should be at least 1.2m (4ft) wide. If space allows, wider paths and greater distances between plants in a double row have the benefit that each plant will receive more direct light.

GROWING ON

Well-grown plants will have at least one strong side shoot at the time of planting. In the early stages of growth you want plants to build up as much strength as possible so leave all side shoots alone. With naturally grown plants, that is all that matters, just checking the plants weekly to ensure that shoots are climbing in the right direction

Side shoot development on cordon plants.

and tucking in to supports any that are not. With cordon growing, the strongest shoot is loosely tied into the support about one month after planting, to form the cordon. Some tie in soon after planting but the strongest shoot on each plant when planted out is not always the strongest a month later. On very strong-growing ground, it may be necessary to grow double cordons. This is when two shoots are grown from each plant up a single cane or separate canes in order to ensure that growth is not too strong and coarse.

With cordons, it is common to remove other side shoots once tying in takes place but try leaving these until late May as they continue to help build the strength of the plants through an increased leaf area for photosynthesis. They should then be removed, as should new side shoots forming on your cordons. Tendrils should be removed at all times because they interfere with the straight growth of cordon haulm and racemes. Plants should be regularly checked for growth so that a new tie is placed about every 15cm (6in) as each cordon climbs its cane. It is quicker to use metal rings to hold the plant loosely to the cane rather than string ties. Rings are also easier when it comes to lowering the plants.

Applying water and mulch

Throughout the early growing period, attention must be given to any watering needs of your plants. Young plants are vulnerable to drying out until they become established. The frequency of watering depends on rainfall and soil type, while the amount to give should be 'plentiful'. Better to apply a lot of water infrequently, rather than little and often. Water should be applied before noon rather than in the evening since this reduces the risk of bud-drop. To ensure continued supply of good long racemes for cutting, keeping the ground moist is important but remember that by mid-May the roots should be well down into the ground. Rather than water at the base of each plant, it is better for this to be applied in quantity, either through hollow pipes inserted vertically when preparing the ground or into trenches running between the rows of canes. No amount of watering is as good as rainfall.

PROLONGING THE FLOWERING PERIOD

One aspect of growing Sweet Peas for garden decoration that causes confusion is the advice people often receive that they need to cut blooms as soon as they flower. This is to prolong the flowering season, but is little help if you are growing the blooms specifically for garden display. In fact, advice to cut blooms once they flower is misleading and there is no reason why the blooms cannot be left on the plant. The important thing is to cut the blooms as soon as they start to fade: do not let the plants even think about setting seeds. That way you can have your garden display over a longer period while cutting no more blooms than required for indoors or to give away.

Shortly after planting, the ground should if possible be mulched to help with moisture retention and weed suppression. Traditionally, old straw was used for this purpose and this remains the best option if organically-grown straw is available or if it can be guaranteed not to contain herbicide residues. This should be placed along the paths and, once plants are tall enough, between the pair of rows. Sheets of woven polythene, which allow water through, are a popular alternative and are very useful for mulching paths. Some have tried mulching the whole plot with these, cutting holes to insert plants into the ground, but this seems to reduce the amount of air reaching the roots and is better avoided. Some may prefer to mulch with old carpets or whatever else is cheaply available. Spent hops are marvellous if you live near a brewery. Whatever mulch is used, it should be put in place when the topsoil is moist.

Where the ground is not mulched, for example immediately around the plants, frequent hoeing is a good practice, taking care not to get too close to your plants. This controls weeds and breaks the surface crust on the soil providing benefits of more air into the soil and making it easier for any rainfall to percolate into the soil rather than run off the surface.

CONTAINER GROWING

Those who are growing their plants in containers will have many of the same issues mentioned above but there are also some special considerations. The container needs to be deep enough for roots to get right down; a minimum of 45cm (18in) is preferred but shorter containers will do if frequent watering is available. Planting distances should be similar to the open ground, around 15cm (6in) apart, but a common mistake is to include too many plants, which then become root-bound. The planting medium should include up to 50 per cent topsoil for stability and to act as a buffer for minerals and water but not so much as to become compacted and exclude air. Incorporating water-retaining granules will help the plants during very hot weather. Plants in containers will need regular feeding and a tomato fertilizer, with higher potassium, is best for this. A slow-release granular fertilizer may be the easiest way to ensure adequate supply of nutrients to the plants. One advantage of growing in containers is that they can be moved to shade when very hot conditions persist or moved to shelter during cold, wet periods. They can also be grown out of sight during spring but moved to a display area once flowering begins.

RING CULTURE

This name applies to a technique that had its advocates in the 1960s to 1980s, before the days of growing in rockwool and hydroponics. These latter techniques are used by commercial growers in association with computer-controlled application of water and nutrients, and have no place in this book. Ring culture pre-dated them but had the same effect, as originally conceived, of removing the root system from the risk of diseases in ground soil from previous crops. Plants were grown in a cylinder, rather like a bottomless plant pot, known as a ring from its spherical shape when looking down on it. Bitumen paper was popular

Dwarf Sweet Pea growing in a 250mm (10in) diameter pot.

Sweet Pea 'Matucana' in a mixed border at Wisley Gardens.

for the rings since this was biodegradable and the whole rootball removed at the end of the season. Other more permanent materials could be used as long as they were thoroughly cleaned before re-use. The rings were stood on beds of coke ash, which was readily available when the technique was first conceived. Pea gravel or similar might serve as a modern equivalent. It was then filled with a good growing medium and an appropriate number of plants inserted for the diameter of the ring. Dressing the surface with pea gravel has a mulching effect and prevents growing medium being washed around or over-compacted when watering.

On a garden scale, the technique was adapted by some people to excavate a hole in the border, about 60mm (2.5in) deep, to hold a ring of good growing medium higher than the surrounding soil level for the plants to grow in. The benefits of this include providing a greater depth of good soil if the original garden soil is shallow or poor, and warmer soil temperature for the plant roots. Warmer soil means that plants are much less prone to bud-drop though it does mean that they require more watering. An adaptation of this that I have used successfully is to provide grow-bags with holes cut into the bottom so that roots can permeate into the cultivated soil below. Ten cordon plants can be grown in a 30 litre grow-bag and there is no doubt that incidents of bud-drop are reduced using this method. This allows late spring flowering of summer varieties, whose flower initiation is normally delayed not by short days but by bud-dropping.

CHAPTER 6

Cut flower crop production

This short chapter may appear to have little interest for gardeners whose only concern is to enjoy Sweet Peas in their garden while cutting a few for family and friends. There are, however, very many people who grow Sweet Peas specifically as a crop rather than for decorative purposes. This is usually for cut flower sales at the garden gate or through a local florist; often they are sold to raise money for charity. We call this 'hobby growing' to distinguish from commercial cut flower producers. In the UK and Ireland, and to a lesser extent in other countries, cut flowers are produced for exhibition at local and national flower shows. Specific advice for exhibitors is given in the next chapter but this chapter considers the needs of hobby growers.

WORLD PERSPECTIVE

The good old grower selling their cut Sweet Peas at the garden gate or supplying a local florist may not appear to have much in common with the global cut flower market but it is simply a matter of scale, and commercial producers are fast disappearing. The Sweet Pea has declined with globalization of the cut flower market because of its relatively short vase life. If there was only one thing that Sweet Pea breeders could do, it would be to extend the life of flowers. Up to the 1960s, there were large numbers of commercial growers in the UK, Netherlands, USA, Australia, Japan and elsewhere but only in Japan does the market remain reasonably buoyant.

The UK currently has just three truly commercial growers remaining. The largest of these

Use of Sweet Peas in floral art.

is Greenlines Nursery near Chichester, where some 800,000 racemes a year are produced in 0.6 hectare (1½ acres) of glasshouse. These are mostly sold via contracts with supermarket chains and through Covent Garden wholesale market. It is a remarkably efficient, thriving operation where costs have been stripped to a minimum.

Cut flower production at Greenlines nursery (D. Guscott).

Plants are grown as cordons supported by strings, in rockwool medium where their water, nutrient, temperature and humidity needs are all computer controlled. It is not the purpose of this book to teach people how to become a commercial cut flower producer.

Dutch Sweet Pea growers still exist, fitting the crop alongside other cut flower crops. Their blooms are often available in the UK. The Netherlands also acts as the wholesale market for Sweet Peas produced around the world, for example Kenya. Elsewhere in northern Europe, there are growers supplying their national or local markets. Other countries are considered as part of Chapter 11. In the UK, the loss of cut flower Sweet Pea growers has created an opportunity for Greenlines to now sell these in season by mail order via the internet. Demand for blooms exceeds supply and they remain very popular, especially for weddings and other events. It has also created an opportunity for hobby growers, those who grow and sell Sweet Pea blooms, to make some money without it being their main source of income. There appears recently to be a growth in the number of people hobby growing to meet the shortfall in supply.

HOBBY GROWING

Varieties chosen for cut flower production may be different to those chosen by exhibitors. The cut flower grower wants long racemes with plenty of flowers placed along them. The size of flowers is less critical than their condition. Many of the modern varieties are raised by amateur exhibitors and will regularly produce four flowers per raceme, but not more than this. Placement of the flowers is relatively bunched at the top of the raceme, rather than nicely spaced along it. Some florists prefer only self-coloured varieties as this makes it easier for them to blend colours with other flowers. Recent signs in the UK are that fancy colours catch the public's attention and these are becoming more popular if a few are included in a mixed bunch.

Home-grown mixed bunches on sale.

Condition is very important when producing blooms for sale. By this we mean there should be no weather damage or other damage and the petals should be fresh and turgid. This is not always possible when growing outdoors in the UK. Growing outdoors does, however, have two benefits. Firstly, blooms can be produced in mid-summer when commercial cut flower producers have finished cropping so there is less competition. Secondly, costs are minimal so that some losses through weather damage can be accepted. Some would argue that blooms produced outdoors have a sparkle and turgidity that is often missing from blooms produced under cover. However, the opposite can be true when petals have been affected by wind and rain.

REDUCING PETAL DAMAGE AFTER RAIN

Rain damage can be reduced by 'swishing' the blooms immediately after cutting. As you go along the row cutting blooms, hold the bunch in one hand by the base of the racemes. There should not be too many in a bunch so that the flowers are not tightly bunched. Hold the bunch horizontally at arm's length and then bring your arm down sharply so that it is pointing towards the ground. This 'swishing' motion should be repeated several times to remove surplus moisture from the flowers. The blooms should then ideally be kept in a room where gently warm air is circulating for a few hours.

A structure to cover blooms against rain can be made quite cheaply at home (A. Hubbuck).

Many hobby growers like to use some form of protected cropping. At one extreme, this may mean growing the crop entirely in a glass or polythene house. This allows heat to be given to keep the environment frost-free and ensure an early crop from early-flowering varieties that will achieve the highest prices. At the other extreme, plants may be grown entirely as an outdoor crop but under a framework that allows polythene to be stretched over the plants when bad weather threatens. In between would be a crop grown in a well-ventilated and unheated glass or polythene house; the resulting crop is less early but is produced at lower cost. Such a crop should be a spring crop to avoid the damage from high summer temperatures. When considering whether or not to use protected cropping, one factor is that some colours are enhanced under cover, e.g. orange, while some may fade, for example if grown too close to the glass or polythene. If using polythene, it pays to buy the best quality of horticultural polythene that is available at the time.

SUCCESSIONAL SOWING

In principle

This brings us to the subject of successional cropping. By this we mean the opportunity to have a series of crops maturing at different times in order to prolong the availability of blooms. Some growers might also fit one or more Sweet Pea crops in a season around other flowers, such as *Antirrhinum*. In theory, Sweet Pea blooms could be produced all year round but the cost and technology involved are beyond the means of the hobby grower. It is not even cost-effective for commercial growers to achieve this. If a heated environment is available, an August sowing in the UK would provide blooms from winter-flowering varieties around mid-February, depending on winter light, temperature and humidity levels. In mild conditions, earlier flower initiation can take place so that flowering may start in December. Such plants should keep cropping until mid-April. Spring flowering varieties sown in September and grown in such conditions should crop in April and May.

Unheated cropping

For most hobby gardeners, the cost of producing such early blooms is prohibitive and unheated cropping is preferred. Little information is available on this so my experience is limited to the south of England. Spencer varieties sown in September, or early-flowering varieties sown in early October, will generally flower from mid-April if grown in a cold glass or polythene house. If sown earlier than this, they make too much soft growth that is then killed by winter frosts. Slightly earlier dates may however be appropriate further north. An October sowing, or any later date through the winter, produces plants that start to bloom in late May, giving early summer cropping. This is better grown outdoors, just covering against bad weather, as cropping is shortened by summer heat if grown in a cold glass or polythene house. Blooms in mid-summer are less easy to achieve.

Two bunches of five blooms each can be presented more quickly and easily than one bunch of ten blooms (D. Guscott).

A March sowing gives little growing time before the plant needs to be helped by removal of early racemes, known as 'disbudding', so that the plant's energies go into vegetative growth. Such plants need to be nursed through any hot weather in June and July by giving them a damp, humid environment. This may mean damping the ground around the plants each morning and at mid-day on hot, sunny days. Some prefer to fill shallow trays with water that can then evaporate, but the effect is the same. Directly damping the foliage should be avoided as this increases the risk of leaf spot diseases. It is also beneficial to locate this crop where it can get some natural shade during the hottest part of the day but also receives direct sun at other times. If this is not available from trees or buildings, temporary shade can be given using hessian sheets over a framework, in the same way that polythene is used against rain and wind. Similar treatment needs to be given to May-sown plants that are intended for early autumn flowering. These experience more risk of weather damage so a protected environment is preferred for such a late crop.

THE CORDON METHOD OF GROWING

Whether growing in a protected environment or outdoors, those producing cut flowers mostly grow their plants as cordons since this gives long, straight racemes over a longer flowering period. The cordon system was introduced in Chapter 5 and can be a lot of work but provides its own rewards. Extra tasks for the cordon grower include removing side shoots, removing tendrils and tying into the canes or other support. If growing in a protected environment, such as a cold glass or polythene house, strings can be used as support for the climbing plants. New growth is simply twisted around the string every 30cm (1ft) or so, while rings are preferred if using canes as supports. When lowering plants, the strings can simply be dropped to make the job quicker and easier. Anything that helps keep down costs and labour to ensure the profitability of the crop should be considered.

The most popular method of lowering plants

Two shoots growing from each plant to form double cordons.

Hoop lowering of cordon plants in Japan (K. Hammett).

in Japan is called hoop lowering. Rather than trail plants along the ground, as in conventional lowering, the haulm is coiled into a hoop and supported on the netting used in preference to canes. Varying the size of the hoop enables extremely uniform plant height to be achieved following lowering. It also raises the haulm above the ground making it less prone to damage and improves air circulation around the foliage.

One technique that appears to have died out in the UK but is still used by some growers in other parts of the world, is to use replacement cordons from a single plant in order to reduce the cost of labour involved in lowering plants. Take a single cordon up a cane or netting as usual. When it reaches 1m high, allow a side shoot on one side to start developing. By the time the primary cordon has reached 2m, the side shoot will be 1m high. Rather than lower the primary cordon, it is cut out altogether so that just the side shoot remains. This is trained up to replace the primary cordon while a further side shoot is then allowed to start developing. This cycle continues for as long as the plant remains vigorous and produces side shoots. The quality of blooms is not quite as good as with the better-known cordon system but is certainly good enough for cut flower sales.

THE NATURAL METHOD OF GROWING

There may be some for whom the natural growing system is more appropriate. This was how cut flower Sweet Peas were produced up to Edwardian times. At that time, rows of plants were supported by pea sticks. Manure was plentiful to create the good soil that is essential if this approach to growing cut blooms is to be taken. The main advantage is that labour input is seriously reduced, since there is no need for the daily tasks of tying in and removing side shoots. All that is required is ensuring that young growth stays within the support provided; an open netting being the most likely nowadays. When using this method, you do not even remove tendrils, though this task is possible. Removing tendrils would reduce the number of bent racemes that are the serious disadvantage of this method. Some unsaleable racemes are inevitable since the plants are not as securely held

Quality blooms produced on naturally grown plants. The variety is 'Naomi Nazareth' (S. Cuttle).

as with cordons and there will be some movement caused by wind. Removing tendrils removes the risk of racemes becoming bent through pressure exerted by the tendrils.

The more work that goes into the plants, the higher the proportion of saleable racemes. If space for extra plants is not an issue, very low labour input with a higher number of losses may make sense. Having so many more plants because they require less work can be a cost-effective way of producing cut blooms on good soil.

PREPARING BLOOMS FOR SALE

However they are grown, blooms should be cut to provide the maximum length of raceme. They should be cut during a cool period of the day when there are at least three flowers fully open. Care should be taken that petals are not damaged. Once the blooms are cut, they should be steeped with the lower part of the racemes in water for at least two hours in a cool environment, taking care to keep flowers dry. Blooms cut in spring should last for one week due to the cool environment. The plant's metabolism is slower at this time of the

Bunching blooms at Greenlines Nursery (D. Guscott).

year, including decay, but sadly the scent is also reduced. Conversely, on very hot summer days, the cut flowers may only last a day. This is fine at home when you can simply go out and cut some more but people purchasing blooms expect longer. For this reason, commercial growers use a sodium silver thiosulphate solution, such as Chrysal AVB, for steeping the blooms after cutting. The same period for steeping is required as with plain water. This product is not available to amateur growers and is only effective if the top flower is not fully open.

The grower gets a better price for their blooms if selling direct to the public. This may be through selling at the garden gate or through a farmer's market, for example. A better price might also be achieved by preparing bunches for the florist so that their only work is to take the money. All these methods require that the grower prepares bunches for sale. Some trial and error can be used at first to determine the best size of a bunch to meet local demand. You need to consider your customer's pocket and aspirations. A bunch of five racemes for £1.50 may not seem very good value to some customers but providing ten racemes for £3.00 helps them feel they are getting more for their money. Offering eight racemes for £2.50 gives a higher return per raceme and may be the optimum price your customers want to pay. If supply is plentiful, offering five racemes for £1 may mean you sell twice as many bunches compared with five for £1.50; thus making more money in total for very little extra work. All the usual forces of supply and demand come in to play in deciding on the size of your bunches.

It is usual to offer mixed bunches, though single colours are sometimes preferred for weddings, funerals and similar events. Mixed bunches are the staple of impromptu sales – how can passers-by resist that array of colours and scent for a relatively trifling sum? Some customers prefer pastel shades in their bunch and some prefer strongly contrasted colours; some will love a few fancy varieties included, and some not. It generally pays to have a good range of colours from which to make various combinations. Another good way to blend the colours you choose to put in a bunch can be to theme around a colour; for example, using complementary pink shades in one bunch and mauves in another. It should soon become apparent which colours look good together in a bunch and those that clash horribly. With experience, this will help the grower to determine the colours to be grown in future years. Some colours come and go in and out of fashion; for example, salmon shades are not very popular at present in the UK but crimson is. Others always seem to be popular: white, cream, lavender, pale pink, rose pink, for example. All mixed bunches should contain some white or cream plus one or two very dark colours.

In Japan, dyed Sweet Peas are popular, though the British seem a bit more reserved about dyed flowers of any kind. White Sweet Peas can be dyed yellow, for example, if steeped in a solution of yellow food colouring. Dying blooms of one colour with food colouring of another colour produces some strange and interesting combinations. Unfortunately, for me these look too artificial but they may appeal to some and the enterprising grower should always be on the lookout for ways to promote sales of their blooms.

White blooms dyed yellow and packed for market in Japan (K. Nakamura).

Sweet Pea blooms dyed green (K. Nakamura).

CHAPTER 7

Producing the perfect Sweet Pea

Here we enter the realm of the flower show exhibitor, for whom producing the perfect Sweet Pea is not enough – they want a whole vase of them to impress the judge. These are always the Spencer type of Sweet Pea unless in exceptional circumstances the schedule specifies that a class is for some other type of Sweet Pea.

CHOOSING VARIETIES

There is no doubt that some varieties lend themselves more readily than others to producing that elusive 'perfect' bloom. This may be because they keep uniform colour, hold their raceme length, have larger petals, produce fewer malformed blooms, produce more blooms in total, or any of the other considerations mentioned later in this chapter. You therefore need the right varieties. One way for the novice to identify these is to choose from the leading varieties in the 'audit of varieties' exhibited at national Sweet Pea shows. This is published each year by the National Sweet Pea Society (NSPS). In reality, there are more varieties that are very good for exhibition than appear at the top of the audit list. For example, two new crimson varieties were introduced just over ten years ago, 'Millennium' and 'Ruby Anniversary', which are virtually identical. Both are excellent but 'Millennium' was introduced a couple of years earlier and included by a leading exhibitor in his Daily Mail Cup winning exhibit. From then, the word got out that this is a good one, and everyone grew it so it quickly reached the top ten in the audit

Blooms on the show bench (C. Ball).

QUALITY OF STOCK FOR EXHIBITION

Care should be taken by the novice exhibitor in choosing where to buy seeds. Having decided upon a variety, the quality of stock varies from one seedsman to another. This is particularly the case with older, popular varieties that are available from many sources. As an example, 'White Supreme' was introduced in 1990. During the 1990s, it was an exceptionally popular variety being good for exhibiting and for garden decoration. Twenty years later, it is still quite widely available but the quality varies enormously. Some stocks have been poorly maintained so that the petals are no longer frilly. Others are satisfactory but the exhibitor may find more recent varieties perform better. At least one stock has been reselected to restore the original qualities so that it is as good for exhibition as it ever was.

list. 'Ruby Anniversary' is just as good but the safe option is to go for the one with the track record. With experience, the grower will find which varieties suit his soil and microclimate and which don't. In the meantime, using the varieties with a track record avoids the risk of choosing a completely unsuitable variety.

For the novice exhibitor, there is merit in buying seeds from a variety of sources in the first year so that you can tell for yourself which suppliers have

Blooms should be carefully examined for faults and arranged prior to inserting them in the show vase.

the better stocks and more reliable germination. Taking advice from other exhibitors may help you, so the serious exhibitor should become a member of NSPS. This is a good way to meet other exhibitors and learn from their experience. Because there is so little prize money at shows, most exhibitors are relaxed and friendly: only too pleased to encourage a newcomer by sharing their experiences and offering guidance. Even if you are only planning to exhibit at your local flower show, there is much to be gained from membership of NSPS.

Most novice exhibitors grow more varieties than they should; after all, how can you resist all those lovely colours? However, the more plants that you have of a variety, the more chance of achieving a good quality vase on the show bench. As a guide, the number of plants to grow should be 2.5 times the number of racemes required in a vase. So if the show schedule requires nine stems (racemes) in a vase, then you should start with around twenty-two or twenty-three plants of the variety. This will mean sowing thirty seeds or more of the variety to ensure enough good plants for planting out.

GROWING FOR EXHIBITION

Much has already been said in earlier chapters which applies when growing Sweet Peas for exhibition as for any other purpose. Producing young plants is the same. A flower show uses the same guidance on timing that applies for any other event. Most exhibitors will have opted for the cordon system of culture, unless on very strong ground when double cordons or even natural culture might be appropriate. If aiming for a late show, it may be necessary to remove the young racemes as they start to appear so that the plant's energy goes into vegetative growth and is not wasted on unwanted blooms.

Two weeks before the show

The time when the exhibitor really starts to pay attention is two weeks before a show when the prevailing weather determines whether bud-drop can be expected or not. From then on, an eye should be kept on the weather to anticipate what it is going to do, so that side shoots can be allowed to grow if poor or removed if hot weather expected. Similarly with watering: better to have given plenty prior to the fortnight before a big show so that no water is needed during these two weeks. If watering is unavoidable, for example on light soils, this should be applied uniformly at the same rate as previously. This is because applying water can give a surge in growth, including that of the raceme as it unfolds during the two weeks. The effect of this is to increase the gap between flowers, making for uneven placement. Optimum placement is considered by one very successful exhibitor, Alec Cave, to be achieved when the length of the internode is 9.5cm (3¾in), depending on variety. Internodes that are longer than this show plants are growing too vigorously, through too much water or nitrogen, and the raceme will be gapped. Internodes that are shorter will produce racemes where the flowers are too bunched together.

One week before the show

Around one week before the show is the time to look at the developing racemes and see how many buds are present. These will be clustered in the growing point or else the raceme may be starting to extend from the axil. This gives an indication of how many plants are producing racemes with potentially the right number of flowers. It would be wonderful to produce a vase of Sweet Peas with five flowers on each raceme, and with all flowers fully open and in good condition. In reality, this is so difficult to achieve that people rarely try. Most modern varieties have been bred to consistently produce four flowers since this is what the exhibitor seeks to achieve. Some excellent varieties for exhibition will readily produce more flowers when well grown, for example 'Jilly'. With these varieties you can remove the youngest bud from any racemes that are developing five flowers. There is a small risk that later on one of the remaining buds is lost so you end up with just three flowers. However, removal at this stage enables the raceme to develop as if the fifth bud had never been there. Removing a flower later, when preparing for the show, is not so easily hidden from the judge.

A vase of fifteen stems staged by John Robson (C. Ball).

During this final week, several other tasks should be considered. Prepare a checklist of all the things that you may need to take to the show for staging your exhibit. This might include obvious items such as buckets, vases, staging material, sharp knife, foliage, dry cloth, show schedule and not forgetting your blooms. It might also include less obvious items: a pen for writing variety name cards, old newspaper for mopping water and wrapping up rubbish, a long knife for slicing florist's foam, a fine brush for removing specks from petals, a very small can for topping up the water in vases, a folding table in case there are insufficient at the show, and a measuring tape for decorative classes required to be within a stated size. Other items that might be needed if the show is not local include refreshments, a camera for recording your success, money, mobile phone, something to sit on, and suitable clothing for all weathers. If overnight staging, a sleeping bag, pillow and a torch may be minimum requirements.

Preparing blooms for the show

The weather will be monitored closely during this period and protective covers put in place over the plants, if available, when poor weather is forecast. Growth will be considered daily and adjustments made to get the timing of blooms right for the big day, as discussed in Chapter 3. Early in the season, when cordon racemes are particularly long, some growers like to place a loop of wire around those developing racemes that will be considered for cutting. The wire holds the raceme loosely in position and prevents the raceme bending over in wind, under its own weight. Having looped the wire around the raceme, the other end is secured firmly to the cane. This is easily achieved by using a wooden, spring type, clothes peg with a fine hole drilled for the wire to pass through, or using a zinc-plated tool clip, spring paper clip, or similar. In cold, wet conditions, some varieties may have a gap between upper and lower flowers that will lead to them being down-pointed. The grower should be ever-vigilant for this condition developing and give a foliar feed of sulphate of potash in order to reduce the gap. A foliar feed is preferred to a liquid feed so that the roots are not receiving yet more water.

If not growing under a protective cover, timing of cutting for the show may be varied according to prevailing weather conditions but, as a guide, it is best to cut twenty-four hours before the blooms are due to be judged. At this time, blooms should be

Bloom supported by a loop of wire secured to the cane using a clothes peg.

cut with the top bloom not quite fully open. They should then be treated as previously described for cut flowers. It is worth allowing plenty of time for cutting blooms for the show if you can. This is not always easy, for example if cutting when rain threatens! Assuming time permits, examine each bloom carefully and only cut those that you will be content to put in a vase on the show bench. If a raceme has faults at the time of cutting, they will not be any better at staging time. Having said that, you should always aim to take some spare racemes to allow for damage in transit.

Transporting blooms to the show

Most exhibitors like to transport their blooms to the show in water but care must be taken to ensure that blooms do not get spoiled by water splashes and are not so crowded that petals get damaged. The alternative is to carry dry in flower boxes. The peduncles need to be carefully dried when placing blooms in boxes and at least two hours must be allowed on arrival at the show for the blooms to steep in buckets of water before you can begin to stage them. Dry carrying is not recommended for beginners. All manner of devices are used by people to transport blooms to the show but the most popular principle is to use one or more containers that are wider than their height for stability. Inside these should be some wire mesh or wet floral foam to hold the bottoms of the racemes. The tops of the racemes are held upright using wire mesh stretched across the top of the container or a lid with holes drilled in it.

At the show

It should go without saying that exhibitors will have made themselves familiar with the show's rules and the requirements for staging the class or classes entered. This applies with all flower showing. Allow plenty of time for staging and, on arrival at the show, choose somewhere with good light to set up your blooms in their vases. Vases should be prepared with staging material; nowadays floral foam has become almost universally used but the traditional medium was stems of the Soft Rush, *Juncus effusus*. Floral foam must

Blooms are said to be left-handed or right-handed, depending which direction the lowest flower is facing.

be soaked in water prior to staging and should be sculpted to fit tightly into the vase without forcing. An inch depth of foam at the top of the vase is sufficient as the racemes are only just placed into it deeply enough to be held firmly while allowing maximum height. Water must be placed in the vase prior to inserting the foam with the water level reaching the bottom of the foam. Rather than have the foam dead level with the rim of the vase, a shallow lip of say 3mm (⅛in) should be allowed so that water can be added to the vase after staging.

During staging, first lay out your blooms on a clean cloth, taking care to dry the end of each raceme before placing it on the cloth. This avoids the risk of petals picking up moisture from the cloth and damaging them. The blooms are selected and arranged as they will appear in the vase, allowing for an even distance between top and bottom flower of each raceme and allowing for handedness. By this, we mean that each raceme is left-handed or right-handed depending which way the lowest flower is facing. In order to arrange an even vase with flowers nicely spaced, it is easier to put all the left-handed blooms on the left side and all the right-handed blooms on the right side. Uniformity is achieved through having the same number of flowers on each raceme. You may be very proud to have a perfect 'five' of a variety but, if it is the only one, better to leave it out and use all fours. If short of blooms, such a 'five' should be placed in the middle at the back so that it does not spoil the uniformity of the arrangement. Avoid 'threes' unless short of blooms.

A good tip for the novice exhibitor is to watch an experienced grower during staging, taking care not to interrupt them. It is very good experience to enter the NSPS national shows. This may seem like jumping in at the deep end but there are divisions ensuring you compete against those growing a similar number of plants to yourself.

HOW MANY STEMS IN A VASE?

In staging your vase, take great care that the number of racemes (stems) required, according to the show schedule, are provided. This may be an exact number (e.g. seven stems) or it may say up to a number (e.g. up to seven stems). If the schedule states up to a number, it is permissible to have fewer, but remember that the judge will take account of having fewer racemes. Having six good racemes and one weak one may be better than having six racemes and one missing. If the schedule requires seven or fewer racemes, these are better displayed as a single row in the vase, presenting a straight line of blooms facing the front. If nine racemes are required, these are generally staged in two rows, with five in the back row and four in the front. This usually gives a more pleasing appearance that a single row of nine racemes. With experience, variations can be tried, such as six and three, and each exhibitor develops their own style of staging. For a vase of twelve racemes, rows of seven and five are recommended for the beginner, with a third row of three added to the front if staging a vase of fifteen racemes. For a multi-vase class (e.g. three vases of nine stems in each vase), the same style should be used for each vase so that all vases are uniform on height, width and placement.

A vase containing nine stems of Sweet Pea 'Renaissance'.

Time allowed for staging at these shows is twelve to fourteen hours so there is plenty of opportunity to watch the leading exhibitors and, when they are taking a break, talk to them. Most will be only too pleased to help get you started. Tips such as how to straighten a peduncle, trim petals or remove blemishes are better shown than explained here. There is a convention that a pair of leaflets is placed in the vase behind all racemes and another one at the front. These finish the vase nicely and are the 'foliage' mentioned earlier in my checklist. Leaves should be cut just before departing for the show and are best transported dry in a plastic carrier bag to which a splash of water has been added and then the handles tied together at the top.

In setting up a multi-vase class on the show bench, consideration should be given to how the colours are arranged. Some colours complement each other well while others clash. Some colours are warm and come towards the viewer while others are cold. Let us use a three-vase class as an example. The show manager will normally have these staged on tiered benching, one in front of the other. Suppose a red or warm pink has been staged as one vase, a white, cream or picotee as the second vase, and a lavender or other cold colour as the third. The classic way to present these is for the warm vase to be furthest away at the back, the neutral vase in the middle and the cold colour at the front. Other factors may vary this. For example, if you have two good vases and the cold colour is weak for some reason, it may be better for immediate impact to hide the weakest vase at the back.

WHAT IS A PERFECT SWEET PEA?

A judge should be considering the blooms as presented at the time of judging and not take account of how good they were or how good they may become in a few hours. Each raceme needs to be at its best at the time of judging and the exhibitor should be aware, when staging their blooms, of what the judge ought to be looking for. I say 'ought to' because some judges are more experienced than others, particularly at local shows where a generalist, rather than a specialist, judge may have been appointed. A judge should be looking for perfection in every raceme, and when assessing its true merits, the quality (i.e. freshness, cleanliness, condition, form, placement, uniformity with balance and trueness of colour) should be regarded as important factors. All imperfections, defects, blemishes and other faults detract from the merits of the exhibit. The quality of the flowers exhibited should at all times be the main consideration and should override mere size.

Judging Sweet Peas at a national show.

For each class, the judge should first scrutinize the wording of the schedule to ascertain the constraints for the class and disqualify an exhibit that does not comply with these. The number of racemes must be in accordance with the schedule. They should be arranged to show each raceme clearly, and single variety vases should be accurately labelled.

NSPS has established a points system to assist judges in balancing strengths and weaknesses of exhibits and this will normally be used where a class requires an exhibit of more than one vase.

The points for each vase are made up as follows:

Freshness, cleanliness and condition	7 points
Form, placement and uniformity	6 points
Trueness of colour	4 points
Size of bloom in balance with stem	3 points
TOTAL	**20 points**

In multi-vase classes, the disposition of the varieties should be harmonious and balanced with a broad spectrum of colours. Varieties should be 'distinct', i.e. recognizably different colours. Judges should give due consideration to colour range within the exhibit. Two or more vases included in an exhibit that are closely similar may be downpointed, although this is currently being reviewed by NSPS. If there is a tie when all the points for each exhibit are totalled, an additional one point is available for presentation, i.e. the quality of staging. Sweet Pea foliage used in vase classes should not otherwise be judged as part of the exhibit.

Turning to the factors that make up the points for each vase, each factor is discussed below in terms of merits.

Freshness, cleanliness and condition

Each flower should be fresh, in prime condition, fully open with standard and wings crisp, keel closed, the whole, including calyx, being of good texture. Blooms should be free from blemish of any kind and free from aphids and caterpillars or signs of their presence. There should be no tearing, bruising or fraying of the petals or evidence of the use of scissors to remove damaged tissue or whole

A very poor bloom. The lowest flower is old and has dull colour and drooping wings. The flower above it is facing in the wrong direction and has malformation.

flowers. The presence of pollen beetles should be disregarded.

Form, placement and uniformity

Form should be true to cultivar and uniform throughout the vase, including frilliness of individual flowers. The ideal bloom formation is an erect frilly standard, not reflexed, stunted or hooded, a pair of equal sized wings forward enclosing the keel.

Blooms with a duplex standard are not acceptable unless they are of equal height and width and lie evenly one over the other, and are not malformed. There should be no other malformation (*see* Chapter 3). Each raceme should have four, well-poised, forward-facing flowers, alternatively spaced on the raceme at regular intervals, without gapping or bunching. The number of flowers per raceme should ideally be uniform throughout the vase when possible, but allowance should be made without penalty for the inclusion of one or more racemes carrying additional flowers, providing the presentation remains in balance. Any racemes carrying fewer than four flowers will be downpointed.

Trueness of colour

The colour of established varieties should be true to the current Classification List, published annually by NSPS. Novelties, seedlings and non-listed cultivars can be exhibited in their appropriate colour classes. Except for vases of mixed colours the colour should be uniform throughout. There should be no variation due to age, weather, virus, scorch, and loss of colour tone due to refrigeration, excessive use of covers or water additives after cutting.

Size of bloom in balance with stem

Size of bloom should be representative of the variety, without coarseness, and uniform throughout the vase. Racemes should be straight with length and texture proportionate to size of bloom without weakness in the neck, coarseness or flattening.

GRANDIFLORA VARIETIES

When judging classes that require old-fashioned and grandiflora varieties, factors to be considered by the judge are identical to those for Spencer varieties with the exception of form. For

Vases of old-fashioned varieties at a show.

old-fashioned varieties, form should be true to variety and uniform throughout the vase. The ideal formation is an erect plain standard but hooded standards and notched edges should not be significantly downpointed where these are characteristic of the variety. A pair of equal sized wings should enclose the keel. There should be no malformation. Flowers should be well poised, forward facing, alternatively spaced on the stem at regular intervals without gapping or bunching. Four flowers per raceme are preferred but three should not be downpointed. For varieties normally producing two or three flowers, three flowers per raceme are preferred but two should not be downpointed.

Best in show and special awards

Judges should consider single variety vases as more meritorious when in competition with mixed variety vases for special awards such as 'best in show', all other things being equal. Individual vases in multi-vase classes have no particular merit so that all vases seen should be considered for awards, including those in single vase classes. Final judging of award vases may be pointed where necessary.

DECORATIVE CLASSES

Serried ranks of vases of Sweet Peas make a splendid sight but equally impressive to visitors attending a flower show are the decorative classes. These may vary, and the NSPS national shows have a very wide range of decorative exhibits, but the one most commonly encountered is the mixed bowl. These are particularly popular with some exhibitors because they allow a greater degree of artistic creativity without entering the realm of floral art. They are also an opportunity to use blooms that are perhaps not quite good enough for the vases, or a variety without sufficient racemes for a vase.

If you decide to enter a decorative class, it is particularly important to read the schedule to ensure you comply with the rules and individual class requirements. For a mixed bowl, the size of bowl

DISQUALIFICATION

What can be more frustrating on entering a show after judging, to find that your exhibit has been disqualified? Judges may disqualify:

- Exhibits that do not comply with the schedule.
- Exhibits where the colour or plain-ness of one or more racemes is not true to variety.
- Exhibits where wire or other support to the blooms is used.
- Exhibits where any staging material appears above the rim of the vase/bowl, except when specified.
- Exhibits in which racemes with haulm attached are used, unless specifically permitted.
- Exhibits containing other foliage, flowers, flower buds, grasses or seed heads except where the schedule permits the use of these in the class.
- Exhibits where the racemes are not in water or water-containing material.
- Exhibits where the wrong size and/or shape of vase/container has been used.

If one vase in a multi-vase exhibit is not according to the schedule, then the whole exhibit should be disqualified and cannot be considered for an award. However, awards are permitted to individual vases other than the disqualified vase.

that can be used may be specified. It will also state if foliage can be used, and whether or not this is restricted to Sweet Pea foliage or all types of plant. Sometimes classes will allow other flowers, and/or grass flowers and seed heads, to be used. There may be a restriction on the number of racemes that can be used in the exhibit. There may also be a restriction on the space allowed for the exhibit – do not exceed this, even by a tiny amount. Some classes require an exhibit that is viewed from the front while others require one that is viewed from all around.

A basket of Sweet Peas with any foliage.

Staging a mixed bowl

In order to stage a mixed bowl, first thoroughly soak half a block of floral foam to absorb water. Most foams are designed to absorb water quickly if placed in water with the writing facing upwards. The foam is then placed in the bowl and, if necessary, secured with florists' tape. Ensure the foam complies with any height restriction. The bowl should then have water added if the show lasts more than one day. You start by inserting stems of foliage into the foam so that they hide the top of the bowl and hide the foam. Assuming other foliage is allowed, it is better to use light foliage with small leaves or leaflets such as *Pittosporum tenuifolium*, *Lonicera nitida* or ferns, for example. *Thalictrum sp.* make a cheap and easy substitute for fern leaves. Similarly, if other flowers are permitted, use *Gypsophila paniculata*, *Alchemilla mollis* or other small flowers. All these ensure that the foliage and other flowers do not detract from the Sweet Peas, which should dominate. The height and spread of these accessories should be sufficient to hide the bare stems of the Sweet Pea blooms, once these are in position, without engulfing them. Try using the coloured leaf forms of Gardener's Garters, *Phalaris arundinacea,* for its decorative effect. However, it is a grass so cannot be used if the class states that grasses are not allowed. It can be used if the only guidance is to permit any foliage.

A mixed bowl with any foliage and permitting grass flowers.

Once the accessories are in position, the Sweet Pea blooms can be inserted. A mixed bowl is usually required to be viewed from all round. In this case, place your best bloom as a standard in the middle and facing the front. Four blooms are then inserted into the sides of the foam facing upwards, so that they form a cross if looking down on the bowl. These should be almost horizontal but not touching the benching. My next bloom is placed behind the standard bloom and facing backwards. Other blooms are then inserted facing downwards to fill in between the standard and the cross. These are spaced according to the number of blooms allowed and to ensure an even distribution of colours. Finally, the whole is considered from all angles and any adjustments made to avoid gaps or crowding.

Use of colour

It is important to appreciate that some colours complement one another while others clash. This applies to foliage and other flowers, not just the Sweet Peas. To some extent this is a matter of personal taste but there are colour combinations which most people agree should be avoided. Some people prefer strong contrasting colours while others prefer complementary pastel shades. Some colours are considered warm (e.g. many reds) and others cold (e.g. blues). Some such as blue and

A mixed bowl using complementary colours.

yellow hit the eye faster because of their wavelength. Yellow foliage can therefore overwhelm the blooms and should be used with care.

Broad mixtures of colours can be very attractive but my preference is for a blend of three or occasionally more colours. Care should be taken to ensure that white ground and cream ground peas are not mixed. Cream will blend with salmon pink on cream ground, for example, but not salmon pink on white ground. Strong contrasts such as cream and mauve, white and maroon, pale pink and crimson, work well. Very close colours are best avoided, for example scarlet and orange-red, pale blue and lavender. Some seedsmen offer their own blend of themed colours.

JUDGING DECORATIVE CLASSES

The judge should take care to ensure that exhibits comply with the requirements concerning number of racemes, permitted size of the exhibit, height of staging material, type of container, and use of any foliage, flowers, flower buds, grasses or seed heads. The exhibit should be judged either front facing or for all round effect as specified in the schedule.

Under NSPS rules, decorative classes should be judged for both quality of blooms and decorative effect with a maximum twenty points awarded for each element.

Points for decorative classes are:

Quality of blooms	20 points
Balance, scale and proportion	6 points
Foliage/other flowers/grasses	4 points
Rhythm	5 points
Contrast and harmony	5 points
TOTAL	**40 points**

Quality of blooms

The same criteria and pointing should be used as for judging vases, described earlier. It will often be necessary to reduce, sometimes quite drastically, the length of racemes. It is not a requirement of decorative exhibits for all racemes to be the same length.

Balance, scale and proportion

The arrangement should be of a three-dimensional design to show off the flowers to their best advantage. It should fill the available space but must not exceed dimensions where specified in the schedule. The foam or other staging material should not be visible at all. Blooms should not be resting on the show bench. Baskets must be capable of being lifted by the handle without disturbing any part of the display.

Foliage and/or other flowers and/or grasses

These should be in good condition, clean, fresh and free from blemishes, pests and diseases. They should not detract from or dominate the Sweet Pea flowers. There is no obligation on the exhibitor to have grown these; only the Sweet Peas must be grown by the exhibitor.

Rhythm

The exhibit should be of good design with a harmonious shape which looks attractive from all required judging angles. The eye should pass easily over the exhibit without anything 'jarring' on the viewer. Flowers should be placed pleasingly throughout the exhibit without obvious gaps or crowding. Proximity of the blooms to one another should be neither too close not too sparse.

Contrast and harmony

The blend or contrast of colours used should be attractive and harmonious. Contrasting colours can be as effective as more subtle blends when used with good complementary foliage to enhance the display. An even balance of colour throughout the display should be seen, whatever colour scheme has been chosen.

A basket of Sweet Peas using three colours.

CHAPTER 8

Keeping plants healthy

Whatever your reason for growing Sweet Peas, it is important to keep plants healthy at all stages. There is a general principle that plants growing strongly and vigorously will stand a better chance of naturally withstanding any threat from external agents. Much can be done to avoid problems by applying biostimulants to help plants to grow strongly, or by applying barriers to repel insect pests. It is not the purpose of this book to discuss general gardening practices that apply to all plants. Similarly, the arguments between those who use pesticides and those who grow 'organically' are not considered, but both perspectives are considered when presenting options for control. Some problems that can occur, such as deer and rabbits, are so significant to a garden that it is assumed that some sort of control is in place, for example providing deer-proof fencing around the perimeter of the whole garden.

On the whole, Sweet Peas do not suffer from too many problems but the purpose of this chapter is to look at specific problems that may arise. These are discussed in some detail under three sections: pests, diseases and disorders.

PESTS

Mice

If mice can be a problem in your locality, your seeds will need protecting against them once sown. Growing them somewhere cold usually means outdoors, and a cold frame or cold glasshouse will need to be very well sealed to prevent a hungry

Sweet Pea 'Cathy'.

mouse gaining access. Some unlucky gardeners have a running battle with mice which involves either poisoning or trapping them. Such killing of mice appears to me to be unnecessary when a better approach is physically to separate your seeds from the mice. There is an old technique of soaking seed in paraffin prior to sowing but I have never tried this and do not know how long it would be effective. Even once the seeds have germinated, the young plants growing away for a couple of months are still vulnerable to attack from mice. The young plants still have the remnants of the seed attached just below the soil surface and these are what the mice eat, leaving the detached shoot to wither on the surface.

A better approach to physically separating mice from seeds and young plants is to adapt the principle of staddle stones, which were used by farmers in centuries gone by. They would keep their seeds and grain away from vermin by storing them on platforms raised above the ground and resting on staddle stones. Each stone is mushroom-shaped so that any mouse climbing the stone is confronted with an overhang and is unable to proceed further. Nowadays, staddle stones are only seen as expensive garden ornaments but the principle can be adapted to your own situation. You can use old doors or other solid boards as benching, each resting on two stacks of concrete blocks so that mice climb the blocks and are confronted with an overhang from the benching. You can also use weldmesh benching, but the mice could easily get through this so a thin board is needed between the top block and the benching to provide the solid overhang. If using such a system, it needs to be located away from any close object that the mice can climb and then drop onto your benching.

'Fuzzyhead' is one symptom of virus infection.

KEEPING PLANTS FREE OF APHIDS

There are two ways of keeping aphids off your plants. One is to use a systemic insecticide. With a systemic insecticide, the chemical does not need to directly contact the aphids but is absorbed into the plant's system where it will remain active. This means that spraying should only be required two or three times during the plant's life cycle. The other method is to use an organic barrier, such as a garlic wash, which will require frequent application, especially after rain. Aphid control of Sweet Peas using a parasitic wasp is not appropriate because the wasp requires a population of aphids to exist.

However, if aphids are found on your plants, wasps may be used but are more likely to control rather than eradicate the aphids. The simplest way to eradicate small quantities of aphids is to physically remove them with finger and thumb. The affected area will then need checking frequently in case eggs have been laid. If the infestation is more severe, spraying can be considered. This might be with an insecticide or else physically washing them off with a soap or natural oil solution. As with all pest and disease control, prevention is better than cure.

Using this method, my plants are unharmed and the mice are unharmed, if a little hungry.

Slugs and snails

Collectively known as molluscs, these can be a problem for many gardeners. Germinating seeds and young plants may need protection against slugs and snails. Similarly, plants newly inserted into the soil in spring, when the soil surface is still moist, may need some initial protection. Fortunately, no protection will be needed once the plants grow away, unless in an exceptionally damp situation. Prevention is the same as with other types of plant. Barriers are popular with some gardeners, keeping plants within a barrier of some substance that molluscs do not like to cross. Some people like to trap molluscs, using beer or other bait in the trap. Chemical control varies from slug pellets to soil drenches, all of varying effectiveness.

It may be thought that applying mulch around young plants in the spring will provide an ideal habitat to encourage molluscs but my experience has been the opposite. The mulch provides a wonderful habitat for all sorts of small animals and this encourages a high population of ground-feeding birds. Daily feeding and the provision of suitable nesting opportunities mean that we have a high population of both blackbirds and hedgehogs, so that molluscs are not really a problem for me.

Aphids or greenfly

Of all pest problems, this is the one most likely to arise. Lucky is the gardener who does not need to protect their plants from aphid attack at some time each summer. Aphids, also known as greenfly, cluster and feed at the growing points of shoots. From there, they rapidly breed and multiply. They may cause some damage to vegetative parts by removing plant cell contents at bud stage so that subsequent development leads to distorted growth. More importantly, aphids transmit virus diseases from one plant to another and this is the main reason for needing to protect your plants from aphids. Once viruses are in your plants, some can be transmitted from plant to plant even if the aphids have been controlled. A 'zero tolerance' approach to aphids is therefore required. This means that aphids should, if possible, not be allowed to gather on your plants in the first place.

Pollen beetles

These are the annoying tiny black creatures that invade blooms. They are particularly found in the keel of the flower where they eat the pollen and are difficult to remove. They are worse in some areas than others, depending on how much oil seed rape is grown in local fields. Pollen beetles leave the oil seed rape when this is harvested and, although mostly preferring yellow flowers, appear to have a particular fondness for Sweet Peas. In most years, Sweet Peas are at their peak of flowering at this time. They do no harm as such but they disfigure the flowers and are not welcome in the house when blooms are cut. In some intense rape-growing areas, this problem has caused people to give up growing Sweet Peas altogether but for most people it is not so bad. No chemical control is available nor a barrier to prevent the pest invading blooms. The most effective control is to place your cut blooms, standing in water, in somewhere dark such as the dark end of a garage. Leave a window or door open at the other end and the pollen beetles will be attracted away from the blooms by the light. This is not a complete control but it means that only a few pollen beetles are remaining when the blooms are brought into the house.

Birds

It may at first seem strange that birds are listed as a pest. Most Sweet Pea growers can spend their whole life without experiencing any problems from

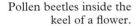
Pollen beetles inside the keel of a flower.

As with all plants, mollusc damage can reduce the leaf area for photosynthesis.

birds. For me, a garden without birds would be as sorrowful as a Sweet Pea without scent. However, many growers can testify to the anger and frustration experienced when their Sweet Pea blooms have been torn apart by small birds, such as sparrows and tits. After years of carefree growing, plants may be suddenly attacked and it is not entirely clear why this is. Perhaps the birds are looking for food, perhaps pollen beetles or aphids, but some think they just do it for fun. Either way, once they have learned this behaviour, plants may be attacked in subsequent years. All the usual deterrents, such as stretching lines of tape or cotton thread, and placing shiny moving objects, are inadequate to prevent further attack. Faced with this problem, a few gardeners have given up growing Sweet Peas altogether but the effective solution, if all else fails, is to enclose your plants in a fruit cage or similar structure designed to exclude birds.

Other problems that might occasionally be encountered are more minor. Plants growing outdoors during the winter may appear as tempting winter greens for some hungry birds. Wild pheasants or pigeons can cause this problem, which is overcome by stretching wire netting over the plants. This also overcomes another problem, which may be caused by magpies or crows. They seem to enjoy pulling out the identification labels in seed trays and young plants. A system is therefore needed in laying out the plants to help ensure the correct label goes back into each tray. This may mean keeping a written record or grouping trays of the same variety together. Having said that, you should not be so fanatical a grower as to want to be without these delightful creatures in the garden. It is such a pleasure to observe them.

Moles

Those who regard moles as a pest grow Sweet Peas in shallower soils where the tunnelling activity directly disrupts the root zone of the plants. Root damage is then inevitable, leading to the loss of plants. Controlling moles in such a situation is not easy. Some chemical control is extremely effective but the chemical involved is very toxic and should only be applied by trained operators. Trapping moles is an art that can only be learned so that casual use of traps by gardeners is normally ineffective. Various ideas have been tried to discourage moles, for example children's windmills, but these

THE BENEFITS OF MOLES

I hesitate to include moles at all in this chapter but am aware that some growers regard them as a severe menace so cannot ignore the issue. For me, they are a wonderful asset to my Sweet Pea plot. How do such diverse opinions arise? It may be a matter of depth of topsoil. My topsoil is deep and the depth is increasing because it is topped up each year with plenty of mulch. This provides a wonderful habitat for worms and grubs to live in, which in turn attracts moles. My entire Sweet Pea plot is riddled with mole tunnels, with fresh mounds appearing daily. The moles do a good job in eating grubs, perhaps helping provide a low slug population. The depth of soil means their tunnelling is well below the majority of Sweet Pea roots. Their tunnelling and creation of mounds turn the subsoil and mulch into a wonderful friable soil. Aeration of the soil and winter drainage are improved by their activity. From 3,000 plants, we lose on average one plant a year to their tunnelling activities. This seems a small price to pay for the benefits that they bring.

Typical pea weevil damage of young leaves reduces the leaf area.

at best only move the problem temporarily next door. It is better to learn to live with your moles and build some raised beds.

Pea weevil

This is the creature that takes small chunks out of the side of leaves of young plants, commonly seen in spring. Although the leaf area becomes slightly reduced for photosynthesis, in reality the effect is negligible and the plants quickly recover and thrive. Control is therefore unnecessary.

Pea moth

This pest of Garden Peas is only a problem for those people who save seed of Sweet Peas. The larvae over-winter in the soil and from June to August they begin to pupate, that is change from larvae to flying moths. The key time in southern England is late June to mid July. The moths lay eggs on Sweet Pea foliage. When the eggs hatch, they move to the developing legumes and drill a tiny hole, which gives them access to eat the developing pea seeds. They live off these and then drill back out in August to September, to fall onto the soil for over-wintering.

Incidence of this pest can be reduced by crop rotation, not using the same ground to grow peas for two years. Some success has also been achieved using horticultural fleece to cover the plants and prevent moths laying their eggs on them. Spraying the adult moths with an appropriate insecticide is effective but there is no control of the larvae once they have entered the legume. Spraying is most effective if a pheromone trap has been used to determine the optimum time for catching the adult moths. In practice, the damage is sufficiently slight as a rule so that most growers will accept the small percentage of losses.

DISEASES

In general

While pests are generally easy to identify, it is often difficult to identify a disease that is affecting your plants. The symptoms of some problems may be quite similar and the grower cannot even be certain that it is caused by disease. For example, when the leaves of a plant start to go yellow this could be caused by a root rot disease, a wilt disease, a virus, scorch, lack of nutrients, nutrient imbalance, lack of water, too much water, and so on. As in human medicine, prevention is always better than cure so preventative spraying with a systemic fungicide will avoid diseases caused by a fungus, though not those that are soil-borne. Organic gardeners must generally rely on preventing the conditions that encourage development of the fungus and remove from site any plants that show symptoms. Diseases caused by a virus can be spread by knife, scissors or finger tips. The only approach for all is to remove from site all infected plants as soon as symptoms are shown and maintain good hygiene such as periodic sterilizing of equipment.

Damping off

This is a common problem in germinating and recently germinated plants. There are several fungi associated with this problem, including *Rhizoctonia solani*, *Fusarium* spp., and *Pythium* spp. The seed is attacked during or immediately after germination leading to death of the seed or plant. Chipping seeds or sowing split seeds makes them more vulnerable to attack if the fungus is present. Rapid germination reduces the risk of infection while seeds left hanging around in cold, wet compost

are at higher risk. Watering of compost should be carried out with clean water. Seed compost should be kept on the dry side once initial watering has taken place. Dressing seeds with a tiny pinch of a fungicide powder approved for the purpose will also significantly reduce the risk of attack.

Brown collar

This term is used for young plants with a brown shoot at the base of the plant. Roots below and shoots above appear to be normal and healthy. Sometimes just a brown patch is seen on the shoot. This can be associated with a damping off fungus but the initial cause is usually cell damage caused by frost or exposure to strong winds. Plants should be examined prior to planting and any that show signs of brown collar should be discarded.

Crown gall

Some young plants may have dense and distorted shoots at the base of the plant that do not develop more than 60mm (2½in). This is caused by the bacterium *Erwinia tumefaciens* or else by tiny burrowing creatures known as gall mites. It does not appear to have any detrimental effect as the rest of the plant develops normally.

Root rots

There are many fungi that cause roots to rot. Root death causes vegetative parts to become pale, dwarfed and sickly. Death of all roots leads to collapse of the plant. Foot rot, caused by the fungus *Phoma medicaginis* var. *pinodella*, has been reported on Sweet Peas in Britain. Black root rot, caused by *Thielaviopsis basicola*, is the most common in North America. In Britain, black root rot is likely to be found only in glasshouses. Having too rich a soil through excess nitrogen fertilizer, or manure that is too fresh or plentiful, provides suitable conditions for fungal attack. Affected plants should be removed. Other plants on the same ground should benefit from drenching with a fungicide. Soil should be sterilized or left fallow before planting Sweet Peas in later years. Application of a fungicide or *Trichoderma harsianum* prior to planting

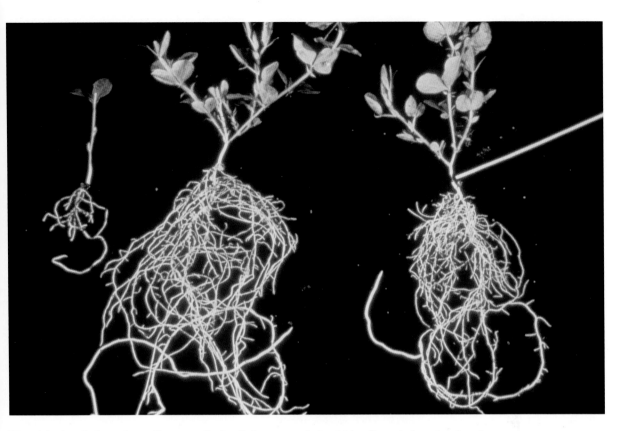

The right-hand plant shows 'brown collar' cell damage and should be discarded at planting time.

may be beneficial. *Trichoderma* is a benign fungus that protects plants by out-competing the parasitic fungi but at present is extremely expensive and not readily available.

Wilts

When leaves become pale and limp, starting at the lower leaves and rising until the whole plant collapses, this is wilt caused by *Fusarium* sp. It may be possible to stop further spreading with an approved fungicide but the fungus is carried in the soil. After an attack, soil sterilization should take place or else leave the area fallow and grow your Sweet Peas elsewhere as it remains in the soil for many years.

Collapse of the plant from the top downwards is a wilt caused by a different fungus, *Verticillium* sp. The prognosis is similar as the fungus may persist in the soil for fifteen years or more.

Spotted wilt is a virus that has been reported from America in Sweet Peas but not yet in Britain. It is found in other plants, such as tomatoes and dahlias. Symptoms are that leaves turn yellow before purple spots appear on stems and leaves. Bleached spots may appear on petals. It is spread by the pest thrips, which should be controlled.

Leaf spot

There are various fungi that cause leaf spot diseases in Sweet Peas. At least four fungi and one bacterium have been recorded in North America. Symptoms include the presence of pale spots on leaves, racemes, petals and legumes. Affected leaves should be removed as soon as symptoms appear and the plants sprayed with a suitable approved fungicide. Sweet Pea spot, caused by the fungus *Ascochyta pisi*, has been occasionally

Sick plants suffering from a soil-borne infection.

reported in Britain. It is generally noticeable on the legumes but is sometimes also apparent on the leaves and stems. At first, the irregular spots are pale green but turn almost white and may drop out, leaving holes in leaves. The spots have a dark bordering line. Legumes become drawn and distorted. The related *Ascochyta lathyri* has been recorded in North America where it and related species are known as 'ascochyta blight'.

Anthracnose, caused by the fungus *Glomerella cingulata*, is reported from the southern USA. Leaves, stems and flowers are first marked with white spots that spread extensively so that the parts attacked finally wilt and dry up. Heavy infestation results in heavy leaf loss and the younger shoots become very pale and sometimes break off. Older plant parts are less affected. Seed from infected plants can be expected to carry the disease but are controlled by dressing seed with a fungicide prior to sowing.

Mosaic viruses

Many mosaic viruses have been identified in Sweet Peas so symptoms may vary but the remedy is always the same. Pea mosaic virus is commonly seen as mottling and yellowing of foliage. Flower colour is broken. Pea enation mosaic virus forms scattered translucent 'windows' in leaves which may also be stunted. These viruses are spread by aphids. Other plants act as alternative hosts for the viruses, including many legumes. Aphid control and weed control are therefore essential to reduce the risk of infection. When found, plants with mosaic should be removed from site immediately and destroyed.

Mildews

Powdery mildew is caused by the fungus *Erysiphe polygoni* and is favoured by hot, dry conditions. It is a well-known disease since the leaves are covered in a white powdery substance but should not be confused with white mould or cottony rot. Maintaining higher humidity around the plant may reduce the disease. This can be achieved by spraying water on the mulch or ground, or placing shallow trays of water close to plants, so that water evaporating on hot days rises upwards through the foliage. This is better than directly spraying the leaves, which may encourage leaf spot diseases. Research in New Zealand has identified resistance to powdery mildew in Sweet Peas arising from hybridization between *L. odoratus* and *L. belinensis*. This would be a very desirable character to introduce more widely and thankfully hybrid varieties can be readily hybridized with existing varieties.

Downy mildew, also known in some very old books as Sweet Pea blight, is caused by the fungus *Peronospora trifoliorum*. Pale yellow blotches on the upper side of leaves are associated with white or grey mould on the underside. Young growth becomes stunted and malformed. Other fungi have similar symptoms, including grey mould, caused by *Botrytis cinerea*, which also contains small black dense masses of tissue called sclerotia among the grey mould. Both fungi are favoured by cool moist conditions. Control requires a change in environment or use of a suitable approved fungicide.

White mould

Not to be confused with powdery mildew or cottony rot, this disease is caused by the fungus *Ramularia deusta* forma *odorati*. The white covering of the leaves is preceded by faint, dull-coloured, irregular, elongated, slightly sunken spots on both sides of the leaves. The spots on the leaf margins, at first looking watery, develop red-brown symptoms like streak. Experience of this is limited.

Cottony rot

This fungus has been recorded on Sweet Peas in the USA and is caused by the fungus *Sclerotinia sclerotiorum*. It is similar to white mould and is associated with high humidity. Hard dark masses of tissue, known as sclerotia, are found among the dense white fungal growth. Affected plant tissue becomes bleached. The fungus persists in the soil through falling sclerotia so soil should be sterilized following an attack.

Fasciation

This is seen as a flattening and doubling of otherwise healthy shoots. It is unclear whether the cause of this in Sweet Peas is genetic or the bacterium *Corynebacterium fascians*, otherwise known as leafy gall. This bacterium is commonly associated with 'witches' broom' multiplication of growth in woody species. Growing shoots that become doubled can normally be grown as double cordons or else one of the shoots removed. Shoots that are flattened should be removed. Fasciation also occurs sometimes in racemes, making them unusable as cut flowers, but I cannot recall seeing fasciation in naturally grown plants, only cordons. No other treatment is required.

Streak

This is caused by the bacterium *Erwinia lathyri*. It used to be a common problem in Britain but is

Colour break caused by mosaic virus is not to be confused with flaked varieties (K. Hammett).

Sweet Pea 'Brian Haynes', a flaked variety for comparison.

Early stages of powdery mildew infection.

Fasciation can be evident when stems split, producing two growing points.

now rare. Purple-brown streaks appear at flowering time on the base of the haulm and extend upwards to mark petioles, racemes, petals and legumes. Small round spots appear on the leaves which run together until the whole leaf is dark brown. Infected plants should be removed from site immediately.

Leaf gall

This is caused by the bacterium, *Rhodococcus fascians*, and has been recorded on Sweet Peas in the USA where it is most commonly associated with tobacco plants. Galls appear on the leaves of affected plants, causing intense distorted growth.

DISORDERS

Blindness

This term is used to describe loss of the growing point in young vigorous growth. Plants are otherwise healthy. It is evident when there is a sudden cessation of growth at the leading shoot of soft vigorous growth and is caused by frost following a hot spring day. This is a particular problem of cordon plants and may be unavoidable if such climatic conditions prevail. A side shoot should always be kept in reserve when training young cordons. This can then be trained to replace a blind leading shoot.

Bud drop

This common condition shows when the flower buds turn pale in colour, fail to develop and fall off the raceme. Bud drop is not fully understood. It is seen when plants enter a period of cool, wet conditions following a period of milder, dryer weather. It is also associated with extremes of temperature between day and night, for example during periods of high atmospheric pressure when very warm spring days are followed by cold, frosty nights. One possible explanation is that the plant metabolism is operating at a faster rate, taking up more moisture in order to cope with increased evaporation during warm conditions. With a sudden fall in temperature, the plant is slow to reduce its rate of

Bud drop: flower buds on the older racemes have turned pale, failed to develop and will shortly fall from the raceme. The youngest raceme above has plump green buds and should develop normally.

metabolism to that needed for the cooler conditions. The flower buds act as a safety valve and are 'blown off' by the excess metabolic pressure. Another possibility is that the rate of flower production is higher during warmer temperatures and the plant jettisons developing blooms as it reduces flower production to the lower level associated with cooler temperatures. Whatever the explanation, fortunately it soon passes as summer temperatures bring more stable weather conditions.

Scorch or leaf scorch

Symptoms are that leaves turn prematurely yellow, beginning at the base of the plant, then turn brown and fall off. The key word here is 'prematurely' since all cordon plants show some loss of their oldest leaves as they mature. Similarly, damage by accident or pest may induce the same symptoms. Scorch is normally seen as the plant's reaction to a nutrient imbalance. The causes are many and complex. No remedy is likely to reverse damage already evident but it will avoid problems in future.

Calcium (lime) deficiency may arise from a low soil pH but it can also be induced by too much potassium or nitrogen. Magnesium deficiency may arise from insufficient magnesium in light soils such as those above chalk or sand. It can also be induced by too much potassium preventing the plant from taking up magnesium. Manganese deficiency and iron deficiency are easily confused. Manganese deficiency occurs on poorly drained soils or where organic matter levels are high. It is also induced by too much calcium. Iron uptake requires a pH of 5.0 to 6.5 so deficiency is apparent outside these calcium levels and on waterlogged soils. Overfeeding of soil induces iron deficiency because its uptake is restricted by excess calcium, phosphorus and other nutrients. It is therefore valuable to have soil analysed when scorch is evident since the remedy varies with the cause. Scorch is frequently found on light soils where magnesium has been leached from the soil to induce deficiency. This can be overcome by applying magnesium in the form of Epsom salts or the ground mineral, Kieserite. Dolomitic limestone also contains magnesium and can be used on sandy soils but its calcium content makes it unsuitable for lime or chalk soils.

The National Sweet Pea Society

Name of Variety

PHOEBE

CHAPTER 9

Varieties of Sweet Pea

At any one time in the UK, there are around 350 varieties of Sweet Pea available in commerce. Within the National Collection, we hold about 1,300 varieties from among the different types and there surely remain varieties, particularly in Japan, which are not yet conserved in the National Collection seedbank. Between ten and twenty completely new varieties are introduced each year, known as novelties. At one time, these replaced older varieties that had deteriorated or been discarded for commercial reasons, but the advent of seedbank conservation means that older varieties are no longer being lost. Although we appear to have many varieties that are superficially identical, for example in colour, type and vigour, in practice each has less obvious qualities that are more subtle. One may perform better in a particular microclimate than another, or on different soils, or the quality of the stock may be different.

In listing below a selection of varieties that are more readily available, or are distinct, it should be remembered that the quality of a variety may be variable, depending on the source of seed. A popular variety that is available from many suppliers may perform differently, depending on who supplied it. Some seedsmen put more effort than others into maintaining the original qualities of a variety. Since the Sweet Pea is an annual plant, it does not take many years before the quality of the variety can deteriorate if more priority is given to the quantity of seed harvested rather than the quality of the stock.

Sweet Pea 'Phoebe'.

CLASSIFICATION OF VARIETIES

Scent

One of the hardest things to identify and describe is the strength of scent of a variety, yet this is the one thing that purchasers are most keen to know. To the best of my knowledge, all Sweet Peas are scented and it is thought that there are several types of Sweet Pea scent. The strength of scent arising from any one plant will vary enormously according to the age of the flower and prevailing weather conditions. People perceive the strength of scent differently according to their own receptors. How well you receive a scent is affected by the other scents previously experienced. Just as the sense of taste varies according to what has been eaten or drunk previously, perception of scent is affected by what you have previously smelled. The wine or tea taster can clean his palette as they move from one drink to another. The smeller of Sweet Peas is unable to clean their nose in the same way. Yet there is an acceptance that some varieties are considered more strongly scented than others. Varieties such as 'Albutt Blue' and 'Matucana' are widely acknowledged as having exceptionally strong scent while those with scarlet flowers are generally accepted as having weaker scent. In the following descriptions there is no indication of scent unless it is generally recognised as being exceptional.

Colour

Earlier, there is an entire chapter describing the different types of Sweet Pea, and we can allocate each variety to a particular type. Most varieties available in the UK are of the late Spencer type and, in order to make sense of their wide range of colours, the National Sweet Pea Society (NSPS) has allocated varieties to a particular colour classification. This is an artificial list because of the many subtle variations in flower colour. Some of the colour categories are clearly distinct while the boundary between others is not always obvious. Some of the colours are narrowly defined while others encompass a wide range of shades and tones. Classifying varieties by colour is therefore not an exact science but the categories are used in this chapter to discuss the attributes of many Spencer varieties. Since the category for a variety may change, only the prevailing NSPS Classification List should be relied on when exhibiting. The NSPS colour categories are:

1. White
2. Cream and ivory
3. Red – cerise; 3a. Red – scarlet; 3b. Red – crimson
4. Magenta; 4a. Magenta – pale
5. Maroon
6. Purple
7. Mauve; 7a. Mauve – pale
8. Lavender; 8a Lavender – flush
9. Blue – dark; 9a. Blue – mid; 9b. Blue – pale; 9c. Blue – flush
10. Pink on white ground – pale; 10a. Pink on white ground – salmon; 10b – Pink on white ground – rose; 10c. Cerise pink
11. Pink on cream ground – pale; 11a. Pink on cream ground – salmon; 11b. Pink on cream ground – rose
12. Orange
13. Orange pink
14. Orange red
15. Picotee – white ground; 15a. Picotee – cream ground
16. Fancy – striped; 16a. Fancy – bicolour; 16b. Fancy – flaked and other
17. Shifters

SPENCER VARIETIES

The naming and marketing of Sweet Peas is entirely self-regulating and relies mostly on commercial pressures. Too often, names are allocated to new varieties that are already in use, creating two different varieties with the same name. Very often a name is given to a new variety that has already been used in the past. In such cases, although the older variety is thought to no longer exist, it cannot be considered a cultivar (i.e. cultivated variety) name under the International Code for the naming of cultivated plants. In some cases, names are changed for commercial reasons to create a trade name. Where these are known, the first name published is normally preferred and other names are treated as synonyms. To avoid any confusion, in this chapter variety names are followed in brackets by the raiser and year they were introduced.

White (1)

Sweet Pea 'White Supreme'.

White is arguably the most popular colour in cut flower Sweet Peas because of its popularity for wedding flowers. It associates well with many of the other colours, lightening a mixed bunch. It is also the most popular colour with exhibitors because paler colours do not show weather damage as much as darker colours. Almost all existing white Spencer varieties have dark seeds, the exception being 'Lucy Hawthorne' (Eagle, 2011). White and cream varieties with dark seeds have a tendency to develop 'pinking', a very pale pink hue in certain weather conditions, which pale seeded varieties in these colours do not.

Although popular with exhibitors, some people have had problems germinating 'White Frills' because it has a softer seed coat that makes it easier to over-water after sowing. It is not really a serious problem but a bad experience has put some people off and there are plenty of other good white varieties to choose from.

THE BEST WHITE

In each decade there is usually one white variety that is outstandingly popular on the show bench and such varieties can also be relied upon for cut flower production. In the 1950s and 60s, 'Swan Lake' (Carters, 1954) was supremely fashionable. Although it is still available, it has deteriorated considerably and I am not aware of a good stock of this one. It was succeeded by 'White Ensign' (B.R. Jones/ Burpee, 1967), which also remains available in a deteriorated form. In the 1980s, 'Royal Wedding' (Unwins, 1982) was the one to grow and this too is past its best. 'White Supreme' (B.R. Jones/Bolton, 1990) followed in the 1990s and there are still good stocks of this available, among other stocks that have lost their waviness. It received an Award of Garden Merit (AGM) in 1994 and is a good choice for all round use. The most popular white with exhibitors is currently 'White Frills' (Truslove/Kerton, 2002), which has large wavy petals on long racemes.

Sweet Pea 'Cathy Wright'.

Recent introductions of 'Mrs R. Chisholm' (Chisholm/Kerton, 2009), 'Snowlight' (Harrod/ Parsons, 2016) and 'Mary Priestley' (Priestley/ Myers, 2015) are all good and popular. 'Memorial Flight' (R. King/Kerton, 1998) and 'Glasnevin' (Harrod, 2006) are older varieties that remain very good. 'White Supreme' (B.R. Jones/Bolton, 1990) is very good if obtained from a seedsman who has a good stock of it.

For those wanting five flowers on a raceme, 'Wild Swan' (Hammett, 2010) produces many fives so is most popular with cut flower growers. 'Aphrodite' (Unwins, 2011) has up to 15 flowers per raceme. From a garden decoration perspective and for general use, 'Brook Hall' (Harrod/E.W. King, 2006) and 'Wedding Day' (Matthewman, 2001) are good.

Cream and ivory (2)

Cream is another very popular colour for wedding flowers and because cream associates better with some colours than white. It is also very popular with exhibitors though all existing cream Spencer varieties have dark seeds. 'Jilly' (Harriss/Unwins, 1988) remains deservedly popular in this colour. It is by far the most popular cream, being good for cut flowers, for exhibiting and holds an AGM. There are now some poor stocks of it around, so 'Pip's Cornish Cream' (Tremewan/Carr/Parsons, 2014) is similar but more reliable. 'Doreen' (Beane/ Eagle, 2013) is popular in the north of England. Others to consider include 'Limelight' (Owls Acre, 2003), which is very vigorous and may be preferred by those growing on hungry soils, such as chalk or sand.

'Martha Mary' (Kerton, 2016) and 'Mary Mac' (McDonald, 2015) both hold AGM and are good for garden decoration. 'Castle of Mey' (Unwins, 2001) had duplex blooms and should only be considered for garden decoration. 'Clotted Cream' (Brewer/Matthewman, 2015) is a little plain but its prolific flowering suits cut flower growers.

Red – cerise (3)

Many of the so-called cerise varieties are close in colour to scarlet. In most cases, their colour does not bleach in the sun in the way that scarlet can. Several varieties previously included here are now classed as orange red (14). 'Restormel' (Tremewan 1989) has long been my favourite, being excellent for cutting and general use. 'Firecrest' (Bolton, 1987) is similar but perhaps not as good for exhibition. 'Tahiti Sunrise' (Harrod, 2006) is bright in

Sweet Pea 'Restormel'.

Sweet Pea 'Hannah Magovern'.

colour and has a white ground at the base of the wavy petals. 'Vera Lynn' (Colledge/Unwins, 1990) has less scarlet in it and has longer racemes than 'Rosie' (E.W. King, 2011) but the latter is perhaps more decorative in the garden. 'Sagittarius' (J.D. Place/E.W. King, 1999) has excellent colour and has non-tendril leaves.

Red – scarlet (3a)

Scarlet varieties have a narrowly defined colour range that is sometimes confused with scarlet cerise, though the two are distinct when seen together. Colours have their fashions and bright reds have fallen out of favour. Scarlet in particular has a reputation for relative lack of scent and for slight colour bleaching that makes it unpopular with exhibitors who do not cover their blooms. Contrast this lack of popularity with the 1950s when 'Air Warden' (Cullum, 1942) was supremely popular among all colours for showing. It remains

available but I would not recommend it other than for general garden display.

'Red Arrow' (B.R. Jones/Unwins, 1983) is good. More recent varieties have been introduced to overcome the drawbacks in this colour and all have their supporters. These include 'Hannah Magovern' (Parsons, 2010), 'Mark Harrod' (Harrod, 2007) and 'Fields of Fire' (Robson/Eagle, 2008). 'Madison' (Unwins, 2014) holds the AGM but the flowers are a little plain.

Red – crimson (3b)

Crimson is the most popular of the red varieties on account of its colour associating so well with other colours and its popularity for wedding flowers, along with better scent than scarlet. It is fairly narrowly defined in colour but has a blurred boundary with magenta since the latter includes the deep carmine varieties that are very close to crimson. By far the most popular is 'Millennium' (D.M. Jones/

Unwins, 2000) but 'Sheila Murray' (Murray/ Parsons, 2013) is also good for showing. 'Ernest Ireland' (Parsons, 2009) is a good bright crimson for cut flowers and 'Laura' (Walker/Kerton 1990) is very vigorous for hungry soils.

'Buccaneer' (Albutt/E.W. King, 1987), 'Rosemary Padley' (Tullet/Bolton, 1995) and 'Mumsie' (Eagle, 1993) remain good for garden decoration and cutting for the house. 'Alison Valentini' (R. Place/Parsons, 2016) has non-tendril leaves. The colour of 'Rouge Parfum' (Beane/ E.W. King, 2005) tends towards magenta but has excellent large flowers and long racemes.

Magenta (4)

Magenta is not the broad category it once was but still varies from cold, true magenta to deep carmine, almost crimson. Those verging on rose pink are now in a new category of pale magenta (4a).

The middle range is a group of varieties that are essentially rose pink overlaid with a carmine flush. 'Grandma Butt' (Beane/Parsons, 2006), 'Starlight' (Walker/Kerton, 2004) and 'Flamingo' (Unwins, 2004) are all very good with little to separate them for quality. Of the older varieties, 'Nanette Newman' (Brackley, 1992) and 'Dynasty' (Robertson/Unwins, 1986) remain good.

Deeper and richer in colour are the carmine varieties. This colour is exemplified by the well-known 'Carlotta' (Carter, 1937), which is still a good variety for garden use. Better for cut flowers and exhibiting is 'Judith Wilkinson' (Truslove/Parsons, 2008), a beautiful deep shade heading towards crimson and with good raceme length. 'Somerset Lady' (Somerset, 2012) is equally good. 'Lipstick' (Unwins, 2007) is well worth growing but is exceptionally vivid in colour so does not blend in a mixed bunch as well as 'Judith Wilkinson'.

Magenta – pale (4a)

The most popular variety among all colours with exhibitors at present is 'Gwendoline' (Unwins, 1999). This is also an excellent variety for general use because it flowers so prolifically. Its dominance is so complete that no other variety in this

Sweet Pea 'Gwendoline'.

The prevailing popularity of 'Gwendoline' on the show bench can be seen by combining audits from the two 2017 National Sweet Pea shows:

Rank	Variety	Colour category	Number of vases
1	'Gwendoline'	4a	37
2	'White Frills'	1	23
3	'Anniversary'	15	21
4	'Sir Jimmy Shand'	16	17
5	'Just Julia'	9a	13
6	'Doreen'	2	12
=	'Mary Priestley'	1	12
8	'Jilly'	2	9
9	'Pink Pearl'	10	8
10	'Mrs Bernard Jones'	10b	7

colour category gains prominence. 'Jayne Amanda' (Truslove, pre-1985) remains a good variety and is popular with some cut flower growers. 'Bill's Choice' (Truslove/Parsons, 2008) keeps good raceme length while others not mentioned are only suitable for garden decoration. All are deep rose pink on white ground, sometimes described as pale magenta pink on white ground. The white at the base of the petals is quite prominent.

Maroon (5)

The maroon category has become associated with dark maroon because the better varieties in recent decades have all been of the darkest shade. 'Karen Reeve' (Reeve/Marchant, 1980) was supremely popular but has long been super-seded by 'Windsor' (Brewer/Unwins, 1998), a dark maroon, almost black, which is good for all purposes and very popular. If this is unavailable, 'Midnight' (B.R. Jones/Unwins, 1986) is good

for cutting and has good scent. 'Pip's Maroon' (Tremewan/Carr/Parsons, 2008) is also good but none keep raceme length as well as 'Windsor'. All these are dark maroon.

Cut flower growers may prefer 'Magnificent Maroon' (Harrod/Parsons, 2016) or the multiflora 'Elegance Maroon' (Parsons 2009), a summer-flowering selection from Winter Elegance series. Some varieties are a shade paler but still quite dark in colour, what I call the deep maroons. 'Burnished Bronze' (Harrod/Kerton, 1994) is the best of these. Other colours of interest include 'Beaujolais' (Suttons, 1972), a rich burgundy maroon that throws fives but has racemes that shorten too rapidly. 'Edd Fincham' (Harrod/Dobie, 1994) is the best of the purple maroons.

Sweet Pea 'Windsor'.

Purple (6)

The introduction of 'Sir Max Hastings' (Kerton, 2009) brings some much-needed quality into this colour category. It has more dark violet in the petals than other purple varieties. In fact, few varieties exist that are classified as purple. These include 'Elegance Cranberry', a summer-flowering multiflora selection from Winter Elegance series. 'Pip Tremewan' (Tremewan/T&M, 1999) is also good for cut flowers but the colour is too variable for showing. 'Solway Symphony' (J.D. Place/ Parsons, 2017) has non-tendril leaves.

Mauve (7)

'Eclipse' (Laidlaw/Unwins, 1975), a good deep mauve with excellent scent, has now been superseded by 'Bridget McAleer' (McAleer/Harrod, 2013). 'George Priestley' (Preistley/Matthewman, 2009) is lighter but good. Other good varieties include 'Moorland Beauty' (Albutt/Eagle, 1995), 'Baronscourt' (Harrod/Kerton, 1999) and 'Katie Alice' (Eagle, 2006). Non-tendril leaves are found in 'Aquarius' (J.D. Place/E.W. King, 1999). 'The Doctor' (B.R. Jones/Unwins, 1979) has darker veins in the petals to give a marbled effect but the presence of pigment on the underside of the wings prevents it being classified as marbled. While most mauve varieties have a white ground, 'Blackcurrant Mousse' (E.W. King, 1999) opens cream and slowly develops a mauve flush, making it an acquired taste.

Mauve – pale (7a)

A small category containing varieties of good quality. The oldest is 'Miss Truslove' (Truslove/ Kerton, 1991), a pale mauve flush that remains good enough for exhibiting. 'Tom Cordy' (Albutt/ Eagle, 1999), 'Misty Mountain' (N. Evans/ Matthewman, 2004) and 'Misty' (Eagle, 2008) are all worthwhile. 'Lilac Romance' (Kerton, 2010) is a delightful colour and a good grower. 'Bobby Chisholm' (Chisholm/Kerton, 2011) is similar in colour and both are good for cut flowers.

Sweet Pea 'Eclipse'.

Lavender (8)

This is one of the most popular colours and has been consistently so for the past 100 years or more. There are currently many good varieties of almost indistinguishable colour so that it is hard to choose a poor one for general garden display and cutting for the house. 'Mrs C. Kay' (Bolton, 1939) was extremely popular in the 1940s and 50s but has now been superseded. 'Leamington' (Colledge/ Unwins, 1961) was the most popular variety for exhibition in the 1960s and 70s, remaining very good for a long period but has now declined. 'Southampton' (B.R. Jones/Bolton, 1978) was very popular in the 1980s but can now be bettered. Darker in colour is 'Marion' (Walker/Marchant, 1983), which rivalled 'Southampton' at that time and has been better maintained. It is particularly resistant to bud-drop and should be used more in breeding programmes. Conversely, 'Ethel Grace' (B.R. Jones/Bolton, 1994) is superb when flowering but suffers more than most from bud-drop. Of all the remaining varieties, 'Karen Louise' (Beane/E.W. King, 1998) is the most popular but none can be discounted. 'Solitude' (Harrod/Unwins, 2014) is the latest of several good Cooltonagh varieties. 'Jacqueline Ann' (Parsons 2008) has enormous blooms and is intermediate in colour between mauve and lavender. 'Gerry Cullinan' (Kerton,

2007) has lavender flush on cream ground, while most lavender varieties have a white ground.

Lavender – flush (8a)

Varieties in this category generally open white and develop their colour as the flowers mature. Despite this variation as the colour develops, 'Honeymoon' (Kershaw/Maishman, 1972) was very popular for exhibition in the 1980s and into the 1990s. It is a truly superb colour and a good stock of it can still be found. Another older variety, Percy Thrower (B.R. Jones/Bolton, 1984), remains very good for general use but later introductions are better for the show bench. The exhibitor should consider 'Isabella Cochrane' (Chisholm/Kerton, 2001), 'Hannah Beth' (Harrod/Kerton, 2005) or 'Patricia

Sweet Pea 'Patricia Anne'.

Anne' (W.Sutton/Kerton, 2006). Also good for exhibiting and cutting is 'Border Beauty' (Parsons, 2011), which has a delicate lavender flush on white ground with faint blue picotee edge. 'Linda Richards' (Parsons, 2011) has cream ground.

Blue – dark (9)

Dark navy blue is a superb colour in good weather, but shows rain and wind damage easily so is not very popular. It is well liked when grown for cut flowers where the blooms have some form of protection from the weather. Older varieties such as 'Blue Velvet' (Unwins, 1972) and 'Pluto' (Bolton, 1977) are unsuitable for exhibiting but 'Just Jenny' (Eagle, 2005), 'Dark Passion' (Matthewman, 2006) and 'Charlie' (Unwins, 2003) can all be used to broaden the colour range in a multi-vase exhibit. 'Joyce Stanton' (Manston, 2009) is a superb deep rich blue and good for exhibiting. 'Andrea Robertson' (Brackley, 2000) is a good selection for cut flowers. 'Lake Windermere'

Sweet Pea 'Border Beauty'.

(Boltons, 2003) deserves to be more widely grown but its small wrinkled seeds make it unpopular despite good germination and growth.

Blue – mid (9a)

Mid-blue is a better colour than dark blue for outdoor growing. It still has good depth of colour. There is in fact no such thing as a true blue in Sweet Peas; all blues are shades of mauve with less red in them. There are many outstandingly good varieties in this colour that all have their devotees, including 'Just Julia' (Parsons 2011), 'Our Harry' (Davis/Marchant, 1987), 'Dalesman' (Beane/ Myers, 2013), 'Margaret Joyce' (Robertson/

Kerton, 1996), 'Karen Harrod' (Harrod/Kerton, 2011), 'Noel Sutton' (Suttons 1968) and 'Linda C' (Chisholm/Kerton, 2001). All these are good for exhibition but 'Ballerina Blue' (Welch/T&M, 2011) and 'Big Blue' (Hammett, 2009) are also good for cut flower production.

Blue – pale (9b)

If mid-blue is mauve with less red in it, then pale blue is lavender with less red in it. The paler colour means it does not show weather damage as much, making it the most popular of the blue shades. Several varieties are wonderful for both garden decoration and cutting and have been

Sweet Pea 'Our Harry'.

Sweet Pea 'Oban Bay'.

awarded an AGM. These are 'Charlie's Angel' (Hanmer/Unwins, 1990), 'Bristol' (Kerton, 1994) and 'Chris Harrod' (Harrod/Kerton, 2008). All three are the standard shade of pale blue. 'Oban Bay' (Chisholm/Bolton, 1997) is paler still, intermediate in colour between pale blue and blue flush. All these are very popular for exhibiting but my recommendation goes to 'Naomi Nazareth' (Parsons, 2009), recipient of an AM in 2008 and keeping better raceme length than 'Bristol' or 'Charlie's Angel'. 'Chelsea Centenary' (Hammett/Fothergills, 2013) has up to 15 flowers per raceme.

Blue – flush (9c)

This is a small group of varieties that open white and develop a flush of colour as they mature. Therefore they are less popular than pale blue varieties with flower show exhibitors, but 'Alaska Blue' (Wells/Kerton, 2000) is of the highest quality for all purposes. 'Dawn' (Matthewman, 1997) and 'Airan' (Kerton, 2002) are also useful for cutting and exhibition. 'Tony Bates' (Parsons, 2008) has cream ground and is smaller flowered. It is an improvement on 'Old Times' (Unwins, 1976) for size and raceme length and is good for garden decoration. 'Flying Visit' (Hammett/Maishman, 1981) is flushed with deeper violet.

Pink on white ground – pale (10)

'Pink Pearl' (Unwins, 2006) is the best and most popular among this very popular colour. 'Southbourne' (Colledge/Unwins, 1973) is an older variety but a good stock of it has been conserved by Andy Hubbuck for exhibition. This is now available on general sale and should be sought by exhibitors in preference to standard commercial stocks. 'Sarah Kennedy' (Sewell, 2002) is being reselected. I have a soft spot for 'Jimmie MacBain' (Brewer/Kerton, 1997). 'Morning Rose' (Kershaw/Maishman, 1980) produces beautiful racemes of a lovely clean colour but has a reputation for not travelling well as cut flowers. 'Lilac Silk' (Boltons, 1989) is deeper in colour. Other varieties in this colour are useful for garden and general use.

Pink on white ground – salmon (10a)

The palest is 'John Gray' (Parsons, 2009), winner of an AM for exhibition in 2007 and an AGM in 2009. 'Lauren Landy' (Harrod, 2010) is slightly richer in colour and gained AGM in 2011. 'Sophisticated Lady' (Harrod/Kerton, 2012) may be better but needs reselecting. 'Nora Holman' (Tremewan, 1991) is still lovely if growing a good stock of it. 'Pink Bouquet' (Harriss/Unwins, 1986), however, is excellent for cutting and for general garden display. 'Susan Burgess' (Beane/Parsons, 2015) has deep blush colouring, useful for mixing with other colours. Deepest colour of these is 'Sylvia Moore' (Albutt/Eagle, 2000).

Sweet Pea 'John Gray'.

Pink on white ground – rose (10b)

Another popular colour for all purposes. 'Mrs R. Bolton' (Bolton, 1946) was exceptionally popular with exhibitors in the 1940s and 50s and remains available but has been superseded. 'Mrs Bernard Jones' (B.R. Jones/Unwins, 1981) was the next to achieve huge popularity and retains an AGM awarded in 1994. It remains a good all-round variety to this day if bought from a good stock but there are also some poor stocks masquerading under the name. One characteristic of the variety is colour loss on the edge of the standard petal and this is not found in later varieties of the same colour. 'Charlotte Emma' (Kerton, 2009) is preferred to 'Flora Cave' (Cave/Kerton 2005) as having more stable colouring. Other good varieties include 'Angela Ann' (Albutt/E.W. King, 1987), which is overlaid with salmon to give it a warmer colour. 'Elaine Paige' (Brackley, 1993) is deeper in colour, getting closer to magenta.

Cerise pink (10c)

This is a new category that brings together similar colours previously dispersed elsewhere. 'Daily Mail' (Beane/Unwins, 1997) is the most popular variety in this category for the show bench. 'Tara' (Harrod/E.W. King, 2003) may be better. 'Joan Elizabeth Child' (Parsons, 2012) lacks the purple base to petals found in 'Daily Mail' and is good. 'Silvia Simonetti' (Chisholm/Kerton, 2006) is very vigorous, so it is useful for poor soils.

Pink on cream ground – pale (11)

This category was introduced in 1997 for two varieties whose only significance was that they are even paler than the pale salmon pinks. This is not a colour to my liking since the blooms appear identical to cream varieties showing pinking. Since then a few good varieties have been added to the category, but it is hard to distinguish them from category 11a. 'Heaven Scent' (Harrod, 2005) is a good all round variety that is worth trying. 'Castlewellan' (Harrod/Unwins, 2005), also sold as 'Harlow Carr', is very similar. Both are better

Sweet Pea 'Mrs Bernard Jones'.

than 'Wedding Belle' (Unwins, 2007) but all are good. 'Lynn Fiona' (Robertson/Kerton, 2000) is closer to rose pink on cream ground than to the original two varieties in this category and is also very good.

Pink on cream ground – salmon (11a)

Much reduced, but this remains a broad category that varies from cream, lightly flushed with pink, through shades of salmon pink to deep salmon. This is a popular range of colours with cut flower growers. Of the paler shades, 'Champagne Bubbles' (Unwins, 1986) has duplex blooms and long racemes.

'Yvette Ann' (Parsons, 2009) is the best of the warmer shades for exhibition, receiving an AM in 2008 but 'Sheila Roy' (Silvester/Parsons, 2013) is also very good. 'Just Janet' (Harrod/Unwins,

2014), 'Tranquillity' (Wells/Parsons, 2015) and 'William and Catherine' (Eagle, 2012) are good and flower prolifically.

Deeper still, 'Princess Elizabeth' (Bolton, 1950) is surprisingly good for its age, providing a good stock is obtained. It produces long racemes but has always had the drawback that the racemes are a little too fine at the top. 'Terry Wogan' (Colledge/Unwins, 1983) has longer racemes than 'Bobby's Girl' (Boltons, 2000).

Pink on cream ground – rose (11b)

A few varieties are classified under this category. 'Alan Titchmarsh' (B.R. Jones/Bolton, 1986) remains very good for all purposes, including exhibition. 'Dream Girl' (Harrod, 2009) is a little paler, a delightful shade and is now preferred to 'Alan Titchmarsh'. 'Anne Barron' (Entwistle/Bolton, 1999) is an excellent variety, especially for cutting. 'Elizabeth Shorthouse' (Kerton, 2004) appears superficially like the pale salmon cream

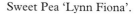

Sweet Pea 'Lynn Fiona'.

pinks but the colour is definitely rose. The flowers are a little small for exhibition but it is excellent for cutting and general use. 'Imogen' (E.W. King, 2001) is an excellent variety with good raceme length but is the deepest in colour of this category.

Orange (12)

The problem with orange varieties is that the colour bleaches in sunlight so they only reach full potential if grown under glass, polythene or if flowers are shaded by Hessian. This and the fact that strong reds are currently out of fashion means that orange varieties are rarely seen. Most have the familiar orange scarlet of the old fashioned 'Henry Eckford'. They are used to excellent effect if placed carefully in mixed bunches but are of limited value for garden decoration. The best is 'Clementine Kiss' (Matthewman, 2012). It is proving to be very popular with some cut flower growers. Despite its name, 'Apricot Sprite' (Bailey, 1980) is a good orange. 'Flamenco' (Tullett/Parsons, 2006) and

Sweet Pea 'Princess Elizabeth'.

'Margaret' (Pettipher/Eagle, 2004) are good but are rarely seen. 'Prince of Orange' (Morse, 1928) has been reselected and is once again available. 'Orange Dragon' (Bolton, 1958) remains available but has small flowers. 'Solar Flare' (Hammett, 2008) is a multiflora with small duplex flowers and poor placement but has the most amazing scent. It arises from *L. belinensis* hybrid material.

Orange pink (13)

A popular colour range sitting between the salmon pinks and the orange reds. 'Leominster Boy' (Eagle, 2010) has a good clean colour. Its large wavy petals and long racemes make it popular for exhibition and cutting. 'Len Harrod' (Harrod, 2012) is also superb for exhibition but a little deeper in colour. 'Rowallane' (Harrod/Unwins, 2006), also sold as 'Jewel', is suitable for exhibiting. 'Evening Glow' (Beane/E.W. King, 1997) is plainer than 'Lizbeth' (Tremewan, 1993). Both have more classical orange pink colouring and AGM. 'Valerie Harrod' (Harrod/Kerton, 2001) is the most popular on the show bench and received an AGM in 2001. It is warmer in colour but does not quite have the waviness of some others. 'Lady Susan' (Albutt/Eagle, 1995) is brighter still in colour and is the one to choose if orange is required outdoors. It too is a little plain but still remains good for exhibition. Do not be put off by its very small, pale seeds.

Cut flower growers may prefer 'Maloy'

Sweet Pea 'Prince of Orange'.

(Hammett, 2015), which is semi-multiflora. 'Queen Mother' (Richardson/Unwins, 1991) has wonderful colour, large wavy petals and long racemes but does not flower as prolifically as one might wish. Apricot varieties are included in this category. Like true orange, the blooms require protection to avoid bleaching so they are rarely seen but cause attention when cut blooms are displayed. 'Apricot Queen' (E.W. King, 1973) is the only apricot available.

Orange red (14)

'Alice Hardwicke' (B.R. Jones/Suttons, 1971) was an extremely popular variety for exhibition in the 1970s and into the 1980s but has now deteriorated. It has a bright colour on a white ground and many have sought to reproduce its qualities in later introductions. 'First Flame' (Harrod/E.W. King, 2006) is excellent and has an AGM but is perhaps a little too short for the show bench. 'Pocahontas' (Harrod, 2006) is a good cut flower variety but the colour is a little too variable for exhibition. 'Flame' (Harrod/Unwins, 2012) is better. It was originally known as 'Olympic Flame', a name banned under legislation prior to the 2012 London Olympics. 'Happy Birthday' (Brewer/Matthewman, 2003) has proved popular and successful for exhibition. 'William Willson' (Beane/E.W. King, 2011) should be more popular. 'Joe Jess' (Hubbuck/McDonald, 2014) is brighter in colour and is also worthwhile for

Sweet Pea 'Apricot Queen'.

Sweet Pea 'Anniversary'
(C. Ball).

showing. 'Edith Flanagan' (Beane/Parsons, 2017) has wonderful size and placement but is slightly plainer than some. 'Dusty Springfield' (Unwins, 2002) remains very good.

Picotee – white ground (15)

Varieties found in this category tend to have a broad band of pink at the edge of the petals rather than a crisp picotee edge. 'Anniversary' (Truslove/ Marchant, 1986) is a superb variety, excellent for all purposes and with very good scent. It completely dominates this category. 'Jacqueline Heather' (Parsons, 2012) received an AGM in 2014 and is also very good but is not often seen. 'Diamond Jubilee' (Eagle, 2013) is no improvement on these two. 'Rosy Frills' (Unwins, 1956) and 'Tell Tale' (Bolton, 1946) remain available.

Picotee – cream ground (15a)

'Mollie Rilstone' (Tremewan, 1993) dominates this category for cutting and exhibition. It has the same broad pink edge as 'Anniversary' and is very popular with cut flower growers. 'Kiera Madeline' (Eagle, 2010) is also superb and a new unnamed variety from Sydney Harrod should be introduced soon.

Fancy – striped (16)

ORIGIN OF STRIPED VARIETIES

Prior to the 1920s, 'striped' was used to describe what we now call flaked varieties. These had almost disappeared by the 1920s so when Unwins introduced a series of varieties from 1925 onwards, they called these striped even though they are quite distinct from flaked varieties. Since 'Unwins Stripes' were the only striped varieties available for several decades, the name has stuck for this colour pattern. Striped varieties have very little pigment on the front of the standard and none on the underside of the wings. The back of the standard and top of the wings have pigment in a mottled pattern and a sharp picotee edge of solid colour. As a mixture, Unwins Stripes was a blend of varieties introduced in the 1920s and 30s. It was rejuvenated by the introduction of a new series in the 1950s. Today, Unwins Stripes are a third series of varieties introduced in the 1990s. All striped varieties are descended from 'Lady Gay' (Unwins, 1925), a variety that is now lost.

A useful characteristic of striped varieties is that they have a long flowering season and start up to one week earlier than other Spencers. All striped varieties are very good for garden decoration but few have received awards. 'Wiltshire Ripple' (Wiltshire, 1980s) received an AM for garden decoration in 1982. This is chocolate stripe on white ground and has small flowers on short racemes by modern standards. 'Olive D' (Owls Acre, 2008), originally named 'Maroon Stripe', is better in this colour for cutting while 'Lisa Marie' (Place/Eagle, 2004) is suitable for showing.

'Lilac Ripple' (Thomas/T&M, 1989) received an AM for garden decoration in 1986. It remains a wonderful variety, but is now superseded for exhibition by 'Sir Jimmy Shand' (Chisholm/Kerton, 2008). This has been the best of all striped varieties for exhibition, setting a new standard for flower size and raceme length. Both are lilac stripe on white ground. 'Margaret Hastie' (Parsons, 2011) is lavender but just as good. 'Lady Nicholson' (G. King/Parsons, 2016) is mauve and proving popular for exhibition.

Some pink striped varieties have won awards for exhibition at the Wisley trials and are good for exhibition. These are 'Ella Maria' (Kerton, 2003), a cream ground pink, 'Queen of Hearts' (Tullett/Unwins, 2004), pink stripe on white ground and 'Olivia' (Chisholm/McDonald, 2014), also white ground. 'Somerset Ripple' (Somerset, 2013) is a good raspberry on white. An AGM was awarded in 2002 to 'Sunset' (Marshalls, 2002), an orange cerise stripe. Marshalls was by then owned by Unwins and this appears to be a synonym for the identical 'Solway Sunset' (Place/Unwins, 2000).

Other varieties tend to not have sufficiently good placement for exhibition but they are very good for cutting. 'Frances Kate' (Parsons, 2011), navy blue on white ground, and 'Nimbus' (Unwins, 1996), dark purple on grey, are both very striking and popular with cut flower growers. 'Betty Maiden' (Matthewman, 2008) is a good blue stripe. 'Crimson Ripple' (T&M, 2002) is preferred for crimson.

Fancy – bicolour (16a)

Bicoloured Spencer varieties were rarely seen during most of the 20th century but pink and white remained a popular combination. 'Gaiety' (Bolton, 1946) was popular with exhibitors up to the 1960s but now only exists in a deteriorated form. Keith Hammett revived their fortune, introducing a series of bicolours in the 1970s, including 'Renaissance'. These were generally only sold as a mixture but he and others have developed

Sweet Pea 'Lilac Ripple'.

them further to improve size and raceme length. 'Promise' (Parsons, 2006) has identical colour to 'Gaiety' but has not achieved the same popularity. 'Route 66' (Hammett, 2015) is more red than pink and very good. 'Charlie Bear' (Kerton, 2016) is an unusual mauve pink and white.

'Chance' (Parsons, 2006), red and magenta pink, has longer racemes than 'Duo Magenta' (Unwins, 2007). 'Duo Salmon' (Unwins, 2009) is a shade brighter than these two. 'Strawberry Fields' (Hammett, 2005) has more subtle contrast and flowers prolifically. The original maroon and

Sweet Pea 'Promise'.

violet is seen best in 'Purple Pimpernel' (Hunt/T&M, 2014) but others with this colour exist. 'North Shore' (Hammett/T&M 1987) is a delightful navy blue and violet but deteriorated stocks can be encountered.

Cut flower growers should like the following. 'Erewhon' (Hammett, 2008) is lavender and mauve. 'Margaret Hughson' (Chisholm/Kerton, 2008) has white standards but the white wing petals have a central pink blotch. 'Richard and Judy' (Matthewman, 2002) is mauve with a dark mauve reverse to the standard. 'Enchanté' (Hammett/Denny, 2009) is a delightful cerise and mauve, flushed on white ground.

Fancy – flaked and marbled (16b)

Flaked varieties have the same broken pigment pattern as some old fashioned varieties. The colour appears as flakes or chunks of pigment rather than the subtle mottling of the striped varieties. Flakes have pigment on both sides of standard and wings, and have no picotee edge. You could be forgiven for thinking that flaked Spencer varieties did not exist for most of the 20th century but innovative work by breeders working independently, notably Andrew Beane in Yorkshire and Keith Hammett in New Zealand, has led to their emergence. They have been slowly improved to the extent that 'Brian Haynes' (Beane/E.W. King, 2007), lavender flake on white ground, became the first to receive an AM for exhibition in 2002. 'Geoff Hughes' (Eagle, 2010) is the best of the orange flakes and is good enough for exhibiting. For general use, 'Oklahoma' (Unwins, 2002), red flake on white ground, received an AGM in 2000 but it is too plain for exhibition. 'Mr P' (Parsons, 2017) is a striking dark blue on white ground while 'Susan Thomas' (Parsons, 2013) is a good mid-blue. 'Theia-Bella' (Parsons, 2017) is maroon on white. 'Pandemonium' (Hammett, 2009) is purple on white while 'Vaudeville' (Hammett, 2009) is the best pink on white. 'Earl Grey' (Hammett/Parsons, 2014) is distinctive in being both flaked and bicoloured.

Varieties known as marbled or veined are also allocated to this category. These have darker pigment in the veins of the petals and no pigment on the underside of the wings. For years, magenta pink 'Sonia' (Hunt/Bolton, 1985) was the only marbled Spencer variety. It has very attractive flowers but must be grown well to regularly produce more than three flowers per raceme. 'Audrey Kirkman' (Parsons, 2012) is the same colour but has longer racemes containing more florets. 'Blue Vein' (Hammett, 2008), opens pure apricot but the colour lightens to orange and develops prominent dark blue veins, perhaps a result of burning in sunlight. This variety arises from *L. belinensis* hybrid material and like others of this colour it needs protection to avoid bleaching in sunlight.

Shifters (17)

A new category consisting of 'Blue Shift' (Hammett/T&M, 2013), sold by one seed firm as 'Duchy of Cambridge'. It changes colour, opening purple but becoming mid-blue. This shift in colour arises from its *L. belinensis* hybrid parentage.

OTHER VARIETIES

It is hard to single out any of the non-Spencer varieties as being better than others but a few are outstanding. 'Albutt Blue' (Albutt/Eagle, 1999), white with a blue picotee edge, is a delightful colour and has most wonderful scent making it one of the best of all varieties. It is almost as large as a Spencer variety, making it useful for cutting, and differs from the Spencer type only by its clamped keel. Other white or cream varieties with a blue picotee edge are not as large or wavy but still have excellent scent. One of these, 'High Scent' (Hammett) was awarded an AGM in 2009. It is sometimes sold as 'April in Paris' or 'King's High Scent'. Other AGM recipients, usually the hallmark of a reliable variety, of semi-grandiflora type are 'Cathy' (Unwins, 2003), with deep cream flowers, 'Matucana' (Harland, 1955) maroon/violet bicolour, and 'Heathcliff' (Unwins, 2003), dark blue.

Several of the old fashioned varieties currently hold an AGM, including some recent introductions. These are:

Sweet Pea 'Sonia'.

- 'America' (Morse/Vaughan, 1896), red flake on white ground.
- 'Bramdean' (Wakefield/Parsons, 2007), a dark-seeded white.
- 'Dorothy Eckford' (Eckford, 1903), pale seeded white.
- 'Flora Norton' (Morse/Vaughan, 1904), pale blue.
- 'Janet Scott' (Morse/Burpee, 1903), bright pink on white ground.
- 'King Edward VII' (Eckford, 1903), bright crimson
- 'Sicilian Pink' (Harland, c.1955) also known as 'Sicilian Fuchsia', an improved 'New Painted Lady'.
- 'Wretham Pink' (Morley/Parsons, 2007), pale salmon pink on white ground

There has been a huge increase in intermediate height varieties since our first edition and the following have AGM. 'Hannah's Harmony' (J.D. Place/Parsons, 2013) is magenta stripe on white. 'Aurora Borealis' (J.D. Place/Parsons, 2017) is maroon stripe on white. 'Bounce Mid-blue' and 'Bounce Navy Blue' (both Hem, 2012) have AGM from 2012. All have Spencer flower form, along with the similar Minuet series of colours, and frequently have twin stems.

Others have Old-fashioned flower form. 'Teresa Maureen' (Cave/E.W. King/Unwins, 1990s) has mauve and white bicoloured. 'Solway Charm' (J.D. Place/Parsons, 2015) is pink stripe on white ground. 'Solway Classic' (J.D. Place/Parsons, 2013) is a red stripe on white. 'Solway Sapphire' (J.D. Place/Fothergills, 2013) is dark blue stripe on white. 'Solway Serenade' (J.D. Place/Fothergills, 2013) is a red/pink bicolour. 'Solway Snowflake' (J.D. Place/Parsons, 2013) is white with a pink splash. 'Solway Splendour' (J.D. Place/Parsons, 2013) is a red bicolour.

In dwarf varieties, many hold the AGM. These include 'Pink Cupid' (Burpee, 1898), pink/white bicolour, and in the Cherub series 'Crimson Cherub' (Owls Acre, 2005). 'Lady T' (Owls Acre, 2008), cerise/lavender bicolour, and 'Northern Lights' (Owls Acre, 2012), crimson/blue bicoloured flush on white. 'Lavender Sprite' (Owls Acre, 2013) is an early-flowering dwarf.

Sweet Pea 'Dorothy Eckford'.

CHAPTER 10

Producing new varieties

It is often thought that Gregor Mendel used Sweet Peas for his pioneering work to discover the Laws of Inheritance, which have laid the foundation for the modern science of genetics. In fact, Mendel's research used the Garden Pea. It was the discovery of Mendel's work by a wider audience at the end of the nineteenth century that led to Sweet Peas being used to verify Mendel's Laws. Prior to that, Victorian plant breeders such as Henry Eckford had a good practical knowledge of how to produce new Sweet Pea varieties, and so can you, but a basic understanding of Mendelism allows the hybridizer to avoid unnecessary work and to predict the outcome of a particular cross. Anybody can enjoy the pleasure of producing their own new varieties.

UNDERSTANDING MENDELISM

The most basic understanding of Mendelism can be easily grasped using simple arithmetic. Most gardeners now know that each character in a living organism is controlled by one or more pairs of genes. For the character to be reproduced from one generation to another, the gene controlling that character must be fixed for that character. So tall-growing plants produce tall-growing plants in the next generation and dwarf-growing plants produce dwarf-growing plants in the next generation.

Dominance and Recessiveness

Mendelism is easiest to introduce if we use as an example a character that is controlled by a single pair of genes in Sweet Peas, one inherited from

Sweet Pea 'Margaret Hastie'.

each parent. Using height as our example, tallness may be represented by the letter **T**, so each pair of genes in a tall variety can be considered as **TT**. Dwarfness is controlled by the same height gene but has produced a different outcome, one we can express as **tt**. If we cross the tall variety with the dwarf variety, the offspring receive one gene from each parent thus:

$$\mathbf{TT} \times \mathbf{tt} = \mathbf{Tt}$$

The offspring (**Tt**) are known as the F1 generation, where F stands for 'filial'. Now it might be supposed that our F1 hybrid with one tall gene and one dwarf gene is intermediate in height but in fact it will be tall. This is because tallness is dominant to dwarfness while dwarfness is recessive to tallness. This quality of dominance and recessiveness in pairs of genes is the key factor that you need to know. If we now allow the F1 hybrid to self-pollinate and collect the seed for the next generation (F2), the pairing of genes is more complicated because **Tt** is not a fixed character and several permutations are possible:

$$\mathbf{Tt} \times \mathbf{Tt} =$$

TT	Tt
Tt	tt

On average, this cross can be expected to produce in the F2 generation 75 per cent plants that are tall and 25 per cent plants that are dwarf. Those 25 per cent with the genes **TT** are fixed and their subsequent offspring from self-pollination will be tall. Equally, the 25 per cent with the genes **tt** are fixed and their offspring from self-pollination will

The range of colours seen when F2 plants flower depends on the parent varieties.

be dwarf. Such plants are said to be homozygous for the character. The 50 per cent that have one of each gene **Tt** are said to be heterozygous and will not breed true. If self-pollinated, they will produce offspring in the same ratio as the F1 generation.

Multiple genes

In practice, most characters are controlled by more than one gene and the mathematics becomes more complicated. Take as a character controlled by two genes the example of grandiflora flower form and Spencer flower form, where:

P plain standard is dominant to **p** waved standard; and
C clamped keel is dominant to **c** open keel.

The F1 generation from crossing a grandiflora variety with a Spencer variety will produce **PPCC** × **ppcc** = **PpCc**; and the F2 generation will produce the following permutations:

PpCc × **PpCc** =

PPCC	PPCc	PPCc	PPcc
PpCC	PpCc	PpCc	Ppcc
PpCC	PpCc	PpCc	Ppcc
ppCC	ppCc	ppCc	ppcc

It should be evident that on average one in sixteen F2 plants from a cross between a grandiflora and a Spencer will have Spencer flower form (**ppcc**) and only one will have fixed grandiflora form (**PPCC**). If a semi-grandiflora variety was desired from the cross, with waved standard and clamped keel, only one in sixteen plants have this form fixed (**ppCC**) but another two in sixteen will appear similar (**ppCc**). It is therefore important when selecting plants that seed is saved from individual plants and grown on separately. That way, either you have chosen a plant that is fixed or one that is not fixed, in which case you select again in the following year. In our example, there is a one in three chance

Flower forms, left to right: grandiflora ('Lady Grisel Hamilton'); semi-grandiflora ('Albutt Blue'); Spencer ('Millennium').

COLOUR DOMINANCE IN PRACTICE

For practical purposes, the hybridizer can use what is known about dominance to help predict the outcome of potential crosses. In flower colour:

- Purple is dominant to maroon.
- Maroon is dominant to mauve and lavender.
- Lavender is dominant to blue.
- Blue is dominant to red.
- Magenta is dominant to scarlet.
- Crimson is dominant to pink.
- Pink is dominant to orange and salmon.
- Orange and salmon are dominant to white.
- White is dominant to cream.
- Cream is recessive to all other colours.
- White is recessive to all except cream.

Be aware also that there are various genes that modify colours:

- Three genes control the depth of colour in cream.
- Bicolour is dominant to self colour.
- Self colour is dominant to flaked.
- Flaked is dominant to striped and marbled.
- Full colour (deep) is dominant to picotee (white ground).
- Light wing colour is dominant to dark wing colour.
- Normal is dominant to dull (dull has more 'blueness'), for example, red is dominant to red tinged with blue.
- Normal is dominant to bright (bright deepens colour; it has more 'redness' on forms with mauve and flaked).
- Bright is dominant to dull.

of selecting the fixed plant. If you save seed collectively for all three plants that appear to have the desired character, this will never be fixed because subsequent generations will always produce some offspring with open keels.

These ratios are averages and, in practice, hybridizers will want to grow as many F2 plants as they have room for in order to increase the chance of producing the desired outcome. It should be clear that it is much easier to fix recessive characters since these are not confused by dominant heterozygotes. In some cases, intermediate forms can arise. For example, tendrils are dominant to the non-tendril leaf form but controlled by two genes (**T-t** and **I-i**). Heterozygotes are sometimes intermediate, for example, **Ttii** is always intermediate while **TTii** shows an occasional extra leaflet.

Flower colours

Most amateur hybridizers focus on flower colour, size of flower, placement of flowers, length of raceme and similar flower characters. Flower colour in Sweet Peas is controlled by many genes which is why the F2 generation from crossing two varieties breaks up into various colours. The colour arises from different pigments, each controlled by their own genes. Two genes produce anthocyanin; another two genes produce anthoxanthin; another gene suppresses anthoxanthin production partially in the wings and entirely in the standard; another gene suppresses anthocyanin formation in the wings; another gene makes the anthocyanin redder; and so on.

SELECTING PARENTS

If you cross two indifferent varieties, do not be surprised if all the offspring from that cross are, at best, indifferent. It is better to consider carefully what would represent a successful outcome for you, and then choose the varieties that, when crossed, are most likely to achieve that outcome. It is most important before making a cross to consider carefully all the characters that are represented by potential parents, rather than simply focusing on the aspect that most interests you.

Sweet Pea 'Naomi Nazareth'.

Let us use as an example the award-winning pale blue variety 'Naomi Nazareth'. Existing pale blue varieties 'Bristol' and 'Charlie's Angel' have a tendency in southern England to be a little bunched in their placement of flowers and for raceme length to shorten quickly. 'Naomi Nazareth' represents the successful outcome of a cross that sought to produce an improved variety for cutting and exhibition in this colour. The parents were 'Bristol' and 'Alaska Blue'. The latter was chosen for its raceme length and more open placement but other factors also needed to be considered. It has faultless flower form, large petal size, appropriate vigour, timely flower initiation, produces good quantity and quality of seed, produces many racemes, and has clean flower colour close to the desired shade. The 'fault' in 'Alaska Blue' is that young blooms open white, developing a flush of colour as they mature, so the more even colouring of 'Bristol' is preferred by exhibitors.

Varieties vary in how good they are at producing seed so choose the better seed producer to be your seed-bearing parent. If the two varieties vary in flower size, use the larger flower as your pollen-bearing parent. The chances of making a successful cross are improved if the right environmental conditions are prevailing. Plants in southern England are less likely to set seed before the June equinox so leave any hybridizing until after then. The best conditions for setting seed are also the best for successful crosses, so the middle of a hot, balmy day in early July suits me best. Later in the year risks the seed not ripening in time.

CROSS-POLLINATION

We have already discussed how Sweet Pea varieties come true from seed because each flower has self-pollinated before it opens. Pollen is transferred from the stamens to the stigma so that the flower has pollinated itself. In the right climatic conditions, this leads to successful fertilization and the production of seeds. In order to cross two varieties, known as hybridization, we need to unfurl the petals of a developing flower bud and remove the stamens before they have matured sufficiently to produce ripe pollen. Finding the right stage for this is a matter of trial and error. The flower needs to be sufficiently well-developed for the stigma to be receptive to pollen and sufficiently immature that pollen is not yet produced. There is a period of about twenty-four hours when this condition prevails.

Hybridization in practice

In order to get started, take a raceme containing flowers at various stages of immaturity. Unfurl the petals on the oldest flower. If there is pollen showing as a yellow powdery substance on the

An un-named seedling with novel colour.

end of the stamens, the flower is too old and has already self-pollinated. Discard this and take the next flower, which is slightly younger. If the stamens contain no pollen, this is the perfect stage of development and younger buds should be removed so there is only the chosen flower on the raceme. This is then the best stage to tie a label onto the raceme showing the name of the varieties crossed. If you leave labelling till after the cross is made, it is easy to miss it among all the other racemes. There is a convention that the first name shown is the seed-bearing parent, followed by '×' to indicate the cross, and the second name is the

Bud petals folded back to reveal a keel that has been cut to release the immature anthers.

pollen-bearing parent. So, if we introduce pollen of 'Lilac Ripple' onto the stigma of 'Jilly', the label should read 'Jilly × Lilac Ripple'.

Simply unfurling the petals means they have to be held back, leaving only one hand free for working. Most hybridizers therefore make a cut in the keel using a sharp knife so that the stamens and style can be teased out of the keel and worked without the need to hold back the keel. Stamens are then completely removed using a small pair of scissors, taking care not to damage the style and ensuring no stamens are missed. Pollen is then introduced from the mature flower of another variety and applied to the stigma. Some hybridizers like to use a fine brush or other soft implement for collecting the pollen and transferring it to the stigma. A convenient alternative is to remove a flower from the pollen-bearing parent, turn this upside down and then place the keel of the pollen-bearing parent over the style of the seed-bearing parent so that pollen is directly transferred without

using a brush. If you do use a brush, remember to clean this thoroughly before moving onto your next cross using different varieties or else there may be a residue of pollen left over from the first cross.

Hybrid seed

After pollen has been applied to the seed-bearing parent, the style is then inserted back into the keel with other petals in their correct position so that the flower can open and flower normally. Some hybridizers like to enclose the flower in a small hessian or waterproof bag while it opens and develops in order to avoid other foreign pollen being introduced by insects, or the pollen being eaten by pollen beetles. I have never found this necessary myself. If fertilization has been successful, a legume containing one or more seeds will develop and ripen. Daily attention needs to be given to the legume as it reaches full ripeness so that it is

Ripe legume containing mature seeds.

harvested when fully ripe but not left so long that the legume springs open to disperse its seeds. The harvested legume should be placed with its label in a paper bag and stored for a week or so in a conservatory or other warm place so that it becomes fully ripe and ready for shelling.

From then on, it is simply a case of sowing this F1 seed and growing on in the following year. All your F1 plants from a cross will show the same characters, and these will be the dominant ones according to parent varieties. If your F1 plants are variable, this is an indication that one of the parents was not fixed. The F1 generation is allowed to self-pollinate and its seed is grown on in the second year (F2). It is always tempting to make too many single plant selections from your F2 rows but you must discipline yourself to only selecting those that appear to be a positive improvement on existing varieties. Chances are that in the following year, the offspring of each plant selection will be variable and further single plant selection is needed for as many years as it takes until all plants breed true. I have once had a variety that was fixed when the F3 plants were grown, a very rare occurrence. This was 'Yvette Ann' that arose from a 'Lizbeth' × 'Melanie Ann' cross. More often it is the other way round and varieties take longer to fix than you think they should.

As the Sweet Pea has a high mutation rate, it is quite common for something new to appear among a variety. Such plants are generally called 'sports' and these can lead to new varieties without the need to cross-pollinate varieties. Equally, natural cross-pollination may have occurred so that the rogue in a variety is in fact an F1 hybrid. These can be grown on and fixed in just the same way as if deliberate cross-pollination has taken place. The merits of a rogue plant should always be considered first, before pulling it out.

When a new variety is fixed, a good way of introducing it to the world at large is to submit it to the annual trials of new varieties held by the Royal Horticultural Society at Wisley Gardens, Woking, and by the Scottish National Sweet Pea, Rose and Carnation Society at Bellahouston Park, Glasgow. At the time of writing, the standard of cultivation and maintenance at Wisley has declined and it is uncertain how long raisers will continue to support this trial.

Sometimes a new variety is introduced which

Mutations occur frequently in Sweet Peas, in this case variegated foliage, which is very rarely seen.

is fixed for all the characters that are of practical significance but there may be some minor quality that is not yet fixed. An example of this is the Gawler variety 'Salmon Supreme', where flower colour is fixed but some plants produce hairy legumes and some plants have smooth legumes. This reflects the fact that trialling and regulation of Sweet Pea varieties is not as rigorous as in many other plants.

SEED PRODUCTION

The same principles of single plant selection that apply when creating new varieties can be used to conserve existing varieties. We practise this a lot in the National Collection in order to restore the original qualities of a variety that shows deterioration. An example of this was the variety 'Geoff Hamilton', a deep mauve Spencer that

New varieties on trial at Wisley Garden.

had broken down to the extent that all known stocks produced a small percentage of pink and purple flowers. Simply removing the off colours and harvesting seed from plants of the true colour produced offspring that still contained off colours. The population of deep mauves clearly included some heterozygotes. A single plant of the correct colour was chosen for its overall qualities and seed saved from this. The following year, it was grown separately but still produced off colours, showing that the chosen plant was a heterozygote. A further single plant selection was grown on the following year and this time all plants produced the true deep mauve colour, showing that the plant chosen this time must have been homozygous for flower colour.

Leading exhibitors take a similar approach in order to maintain the quality of their stocks of a variety. Seed is saved only from the best plants, taking account of all characters of the plant. It is easy and good fun to save your own Sweet Pea seed but most people quickly find the quality of their stock of a variety has deteriorated because they have not been sufficiently rigorous in the choice of seed plants. Saving seed from a small population of plants increases the risk of a minor fault being overlooked so it is less work and generally better to allow a specialist to do this work for you and buy your seed from them. As a general rule, the smaller the supplier, the more likelihood of getting seed from a good stock but there are also some examples of seedsmen who have small businesses because they are not very good.

Only some of the very top exhibitors with decades of experience take the trouble to save seed for their own use, and this will be limited to Spencer varieties. The next best option for most gardeners is to buy seed from one of the few specialist Sweet Pea seedsmen who produce their own seed in the UK. Larger Sweet Pea specialists have their seed grown for them, frequently in New Zealand, where they have no direct control over plant selection. The grower is paid for the quantity of seed produced rather than the quality of the stock it comes from but a good seedsman should be producing at home the core stock from which this is grown. Then there are the generalist seedsmen who are large companies that buy in seed of all sorts of flowers and vegetables from around the world and put it in their own packets. The best will have had their Sweet Peas grown for them under contract but there is usually no way for the gardener to know the origin of the seed crop.

Field scale seed production, unsupported to allow mechanical harvesting (K. Hammett).

CHAPTER 11

Sweet Peas around the world

A testimony to the extent that the Sweet Pea is known and loved around the world is the number of common names attributed to *Lathyrus odoratus*. Many people know these lovely flowers simply by the name Sweet Pea, including the Japanese. Dozens of other names are found, including:

Pois de Senteur – France
Duftwicke – Germany
Pisello d'Odore – Italy
Ervilha de Cheiro – Portugal, Brazil
Guisante de Olor; Zarza del Naranjo – Spain
Alberjilla de Olor – Argentina

The guidance written in this book is mainly based on experience of growing Sweet Peas in England. Growing conditions vary even in the UK; for example, growing in northern Scotland will be similar to Scandinavia and very different to lowland southern England. Altitude, proximity to the sea, and exposure to frost and winds, all have an impact on how to grow Sweet Peas so that every garden is different. The key variables are minimum winter temperatures and maximum summer temperatures. The following notes are intended to help people adapt my guidance to local conditions in other parts of the world.

NORTH AMERICA

It is not clear when the Sweet Pea was first introduced into North America but it is thought to have been brought to the colonies on its first wave of popularity in England. It must have been well known by 1760 because an enterprising milliner in Boston advertised Sweet Pea seeds for sale in

OPPOSITE: Sweet Pea 'Senator'.

Cordon Sweet Peas at the Panama Pacific International Exhibition, San Francisco, 1915.

SWEET PEAS CANNOT BE EATEN

Despite the popularity of *Lathyrus odoratus*, known as Sweet Peas in the USA since the eighteenth century, in some parts of the USA there has been a recent trend to use the name Sweet Pea for the edible Garden Pea, *Pisum sativum*, also known as the English Pea, Edible-podded Pea and Snow Pea. The internet is now full of advice on how to grow and cook Sweet Peas. People should be absolutely clear: Sweet Peas and other *Lathyrus* contain toxins and may be harmful if eaten. Edible peas are a different species and rightfully remain a popular vegetable. However sweet Garden Peas taste, please don't fool anyone into thinking they can eat Sweet Peas.

March 1760 as part of a promotion for spring bonnets. In 1804, Bernard McMahon, seedsman of Philadelphia, lists the wild type, purple, white, 'Painted Lady', blue and scarlet. Edwin Sayers' *American Flower Garden Companion* of 1838 lists 'Painted Lady', white, purple, scarlet and striped. James Vick's catalogue of 1871 lists scarlet, scarlet striped with white, white, purple striped with white, 'Painted Lady', 'Blue Edged', black, black with light blue and 'Scarlet Invincible'.

The first variety actually raised in North America was 'Blanche Ferry', which was the result of unconscious selection over forty years from 'Painted Lady' by a quarryman's wife. This resulted in the first early flowering variety. It was introduced in 1889 by D.M. Ferry and Co. Other varieties from various seedsmen quickly followed. Although American gardeners were behind the British in improving the Sweet Pea, their enthusiasm for the flower preceded its popularity in Britain. The first Eckford introductions sold more readily in America than they did in Britain and the flower was taken up with enthusiasm by seedsmen such as Burpee, Henderson, Morse and Vaughan.

By 1910, California was growing 1,000 acres of Sweet Peas for seed. Problems arose in 1916 when root rot disease became prevalent, especially in those states with hot summers. Fortunately the cooler area of the California coast, which produced seed for the rest of the world, was unaffected. The demand for Sweet Peas in the USA fell off dramatically and subsequent development of new Sweet Pea varieties in North America has focused on those types adapted to hotter summers.

North America has an enormously diverse range of different climates, so it is beyond the scope of this book to cover all options but the following regional reviews should give some guidance that can be adapted through trial and error to meet local circumstances. Both proximity to the coast and altitude have an enormous effect on growing requirements. It should be clear from earlier chapters that best results arise if seeds are sown so that they have a long growing time in cold weather.

Hot summers and mild winters

Includes southern USA. Plants can be started in a similar manner to the UK. Seeds are best sown in October or November once the weather cools but can be sown any time through the winter. Plants should be grown cold and slow so that they are ready for planting in early spring. Mid-day shade will help plants through the winter in the hottest areas, such as Texas and Florida. The effect of summer heat may be reduced by deep mulching, particularly in drier states. Early flowering and dwarf varieties may do better in these hottest areas. Early varieties can also be sown in late summer and grown to flower for Christmas.

Moderate summers and moderate winters

In areas such as coastal British Columbia and Oregon, at higher altitude in the more southerly states, and some coastal areas of the northeast, all types of Sweet Peas may be grown just as they are in the UK. Sowing can take place any time from October through to spring and there is little to add to the guidance elsewhere in this book.

Hot summer temperatures can induce bizarre growth in Winter Elegance series. In this case, the end of the raceme has converted into a vegetative shoot.

Hot summers and cold winters

Includes areas such as the mid-Atlantic states, northern non-coastal areas and the Mid-West. These areas are at risk of frosts but hot, humid, summer weather can come early. Here, seeds are best sown indoors six or eight weeks before the last frost and moved to a cold temperature area once germinated – remember plants are frost-tolerant.

Again, the effect of summer heat may be reduced by deep mulching. Early flowering and dwarf varieties may do better in these areas.

Very cold winters

Includes New England. Seed is sown six weeks before the last hard frost, perhaps sowing in late March, depending on locality. All types can be

Sweet Pea 'Riga 800' raised by Martin Maltenieks in Latvia (M. Maltenieks).

grown here though flowering will be later than in the UK. If summers are hot, planting to provide some light mid-day shade is beneficial.

EUROPE

Sweet Peas were introduced into the Netherlands at the same time as England and may have been grown elsewhere in Europe from this very early time. However, I am not aware of any documents recording Sweet Peas in France and Germany until around a hundred years later. Nowadays, Sweet Peas are grown for cut flowers to meet local markets throughout Europe. Dutch domination in the global cut flower industry means that production there is high and there is a Dutch Sweet Pea society, Nederlandse Lathyrus Vereniging. In recent years, one Dutch grower has relocated production to Kenya. Factors for those growing in Europe's variable climate are the same as for North America. Account needs to be taken of areas with colder winters than the UK or with hotter summers, but otherwise the guidance in this book will be generally applicable.

AUSTRALIA

It is not known exactly when Sweet Peas were first imported into Australia. Mrs John Busby brought 'Painted Lady' into New South Wales (NSW) in 1823. This has been maintained by the family through many generations until its history was recorded and seed made available through the Australian Garden History Society. It is now sold as 'The Busby Pea' to distinguish it from other varieties of this colouring.

Cultivation is almost entirely limited to the cooler, coastal areas. The early part of the twentieth century saw considerable interest in Sweet Pea cultivation and from 1903 there was a Carnation and Sweet Pea Society in South Australia. The Spencer type must have been imported early into Australia because an early-flowering variety of this, 'Yarrawa', had arisen by 1909. Many Australian seedsmen were involved in the creation of new varieties, with shared interest between Australia and the USA in the early-flowering types. Considerable hybridizing was done up to the early 1950s to improve the traditional Early Spencer types but Australian varieties were gradually superseded by American varieties. Among the specialist Australian growers were Eric Carter and J. Harkness of South Australia, Queale of Victoria, and W. Steward and J.F. Scobie of NSW. Perhaps most famous of all is Arthur Yates of NSW who

Sweet Pea 'Pink Cupid' being grown for seed in California (K. Hammett).

introduced 'Yarrawa' and whose company is still important.

By 1975, Early Multiflora Gigantea series had largely replaced all other types throughout Australia. Spring-flowering types have also been imported but the English summer Spencer varieties are virtually unknown. Cuthbertson Floribunda series were imported and these did particularly well in Victoria and Tasmania, now superseded by Royal series. Commercial cut flower production has waned over the years but the distinctive Gawler series remains, maintained in commercial cultivation by the McDougall family of South Australia.

Growing Sweet Peas in Australia is best left to the early-flowering types because of summer heat, although summer-flowering types may be successful in Tasmania and at altitude where summers are not too hot. The regional information given under North America could also be helpful for Australian growers, recognizing of course that reference to seasons remains the same (spring is still spring) but references to months should be changed (e.g. for October read April, and so on). In fact the McDougalls recommend sowing in mid- to late March.

JAPAN

Sweet Peas are very popular with Japanese people who particularly welcome cut flowers during

Competitive classes at Miyazaki flower festival
(K. Nakamura).

winter to help them think that spring will come
soon. Early season Sweet Peas are also preferred
to summer-flowering because of the climate. After
April, temperatures get too high and June and July
are the rainy season. Generally, seeds are sown in
August/September with cut flower production in
glass or polythene houses from November to April.
Spring-flowering varieties are given pre-sowing
cold treatment to produce flowers in winter, and
this may begin in July.

Cut flower production is therefore more prominent than growing Sweet Peas for garden decoration. Dyed flowers are popular. The buoyant cut
flower market supports considerable research into
growing methods and new varieties are raised.
There is considerable rivalry between different
areas of cut flower production and varieties are
jealously guarded within the area that raised them.
Obtaining seed of Japanese varieties is therefore extremely difficult. There is much that the
Japanese growers could teach the rest of the world
but language provides a barrier.

ELSEWHERE

Although first class Sweet Pea seed is produced in
New Zealand for export, the domestic market is
small. Sweet Peas were grown in the Dunedin area
by the 1880s, perhaps earlier. Summer-flowering
varieties grow here readily and much of the guidance in this book is equally applicable to New
Zealand. All that is needed is to change any references to months to allow for the different hemisphere (i.e. spring is still spring but for April read
October, and so on).

There was a spurious report in the 1980s that
the Sweet Pea grows wild in China but this was a
garden escape. In recent years, commercial seed
production has started in Inner Mongolia and the
quality of this may improve in a short space of
time.

Leaving aside the spurious claim that the
Spaniards introduced the Sweet Pea into South
America in the sixteenth century, there is a reference to its cultivation in Chile in 1846 and it may
have been introduced earlier.

Wherever the British Empire went, they took
their Sweet Peas with them. Writers of a hundred
years ago refer to the cultivation in Canada, West
Indies, South Africa, St. Helena, Gold Coast (now
Ghana), Ceylon (now Sri Lanka), West Bengal,
Burma and New Guinea, among other places. It
is beyond the scope of this book, and my experience, to describe how they may be grown in every
country and it would be terribly repetitious. St.
Helena provides a good case study though. It is on
the equator and Sweet Peas can be grown throughout the year because of even day length and the
cooling effect of the ocean. There is no reason why
Sweet Peas could not be brought into flower any-
where at any time given sufficient artificial control
of the growing environment: lighting, temperature
and humidity. What prevents this is the prohibitive
cost.

Seed production in New Zealand (K.Hammett).

CHAPTER 12

Other *Lathyrus* species

We have already noted in Chapter three that the Sweet Pea is known botanically as *Lathyrus odoratus*. This means that all the different forms and colours of Sweet Pea are a single species of the genus *Lathyrus*. In 1848, Godron united *Lathyrus* and *Orobus* for the first time to form the *Lathyrus* genus we know today. There is currently no monograph of the genus. There are around 160 *Lathyrus* species, originating throughout the temperate northern hemisphere and extending into tropical east Africa and South America. A little over half are currently in cultivation in the UK. There are many species that appear to be desirable but are not cultivated. Some are difficult to grow, however attractive their flowers may appear. Others may simply have not been introduced, often coming from areas such as Iraq, which makes finding and introducing them unlikely for now. On the other hand, some species in cultivation are only of interest to botanic gardens and other collections, being of little decorative value.

There are a number of reasons for including these other *Lathyrus* species in a book about Sweet Peas. Some of the species are often referred to as perennial Sweet Peas, even though they have no scent and are therefore not 'sweet'. In fact most other *Lathyrus* species have no scent but they have a range of other qualities that make many of them worthy of a place in the garden. They include a range of colours that are not found in *L. odoratus*, such as yellow and a true blue. They are useful for their decorative effect, both in the garden and as cut flowers. Although usually smaller than Sweet Pea flowers, there are classes for them at National

L. chloranthus 'Lemonade' (M. Thornhill).

Sweet Pea Society shows and they can be useful in miniature and petite flower arrangements. Some have been hybridized with Sweet Peas, albeit rarely, to produce hybrid varieties that are sold as Sweet Peas. Hybridization between species is extremely rare and usually only achieved in a laboratory. Where hybridization occurs, subsequent generations segregate into one or other parent.

HOW TO GROW

Propagation is normally by seed or division. Some species have been propagated using softwood cuttings but these require a mist bench or similar specialist equipment to be successful. Species with erect haulm and leaves with more than one pair of leaflets are woodland, while the rest grow best in sun and well-drained soil. As with all plants, a good guide is to understand their natural habitat and try to reproduce it.

Annuals are produced from seed and are normally sown in spring in the UK. Most are quick to germinate and flower, so they respond well to successional sowing to achieve flowering at different times. An autumn sowing will provide blooms in May. Two species that are better sown in autumn because they are slower to germinate and produce flowers are *L. chloranthus* and *L. paranensis*. All require the removal of dead flower heads and watering during dry spells to prolong flowering. Most species do best in full sun but some of the more delicate annuals and the South American climbers seem to benefit from light shade during the mid-day sun.

Perennials may be bought as young plants (*L. grandiflorus* is only available this way) or grown

L. rotundifolius grown as a column to hide an old post.

from seed. The more popular species, such as *L. latifolius* and *L. vernus*, germinate quickly but others may take several months, even years. Perennials seem to prefer a well-drained soil, even if they are moisture lovers. They do not like cold, wet soils. Garden compost, or some other form of humus, should be added to the soil when planting, unless the soil type makes this unnecessary. Many

L. aphaca supported by wire netting.

and sets seeds without the flower fully developing. Several species produce flowers underground, notably *L. amphicarpos*. *L. aphaca* has leaves reduced to a single tendril and the hastate stipules function as leaves.

The species descriptions below generally include the species name, author and date first described, common name in English, and occasionally any synonyms likely to be encountered. Those involved in botanical research will find many synonyms exist for most species.

CLIMBING ANNUALS

Closest to the Sweet Pea are the other climbing annuals. This group is most rewarding and much of my work has been to re-select and maintain superior forms of these for cut flowers. They can be allowed to sprawl but do better if given support. In choosing which to grow, the number of blooms per flower spike, size of the individual flower and length of flower spike, should all be taken into account. They are hardy annuals and easy to grow in a wide range of colours.

L. odoratus *(Linnaeus, 1753)*

This is the 'Wild Sweet Pea' from Sicily and perhaps also Southern Italy. It grows 0.5m to 1m high and produces two or three sweetly scented, maroon and violet bicoloured flowers, up to 35mm across, on each raceme, which is 12–20cm long. This species has a high rate of mutation and thousands of horticultural varieties have been produced of which at least 1,000 currently exist. Many of these are detailed elsewhere in this book.

L. belinensis *(Maxted and Goyder, 1988)*

Closest to the Sweet Pea is the 'Belin Pea', native to the Antalaya region of Turkey and only discovered in 1987. It is found on rocky limestone hillsides and margins of cultivated land. In cultivation it grows up to 1.8m. This delightful species has up to four flowers per raceme. The raceme is reported to be up to 28cm long in the wild but is much shorter in cultivation. The red and yellow

perennials spread by stolons and can be increased by division in the spring.

The fun with any gardening is to try something different and see how it works for you. This chapter describes those species that people are more likely to come across as plants or in seed catalogues, or should seek out. The genus *Lathyrus* provides a wide range of forms and can be very rewarding. There are also some real botanical curiosities that are not detailed here as they have little decorative value. *L. gloeospermus* is cleistogamous, in other words the plant is self-fertile

L. belinensis growing in a container.

bicoloured flowers are said to be scented when grown in very warm conditions, such as a conservatory. It is very easy to grow. Sometimes found in seed catalogues as 'Goldmine' and incorrectly described as perennial. It has been hybridized with *L. odoratus* 'Mrs Collier' to produce Sweet Pea varieties with some interesting and novel qualities.

L. chloranthus *(Boissier and Balansa, 1859)*

Also very decorative, *L. chloranthus* is native to central and eastern Turkey, Armenia, Caucasus, northern Iraq and Iran. It is found on banks and scrub by streams, igneous slopes, cultivated land, meadows, oak forest and hedges to 1800m altitude. This species grows up to 1.8m high and has attractive downy foliage. The raceme has up to four flowers, each up to 20mm wide. Flower colour is basically a lime green-yellow, the standards sometimes splashed with varying amounts of red. 'Lemonade' is a good form with pure lime green-yellow petals and long racemes. This species is slower to germinate and to initiate flowers compared with a Sweet Pea so it benefits from growing as an autumn-sown Sweet Pea to start flowering in July.

L. paranensis *(Burkart, 1935)*

This native of Argentina, Uruguay and Brazil is found in marshes, and is another species that benefits from autumn sowing. The seeds produce tall climbing glaucous plants. It has two to nine violet blue flowers per raceme, and the racemes are 15–35cm long. A white-flowered form has been described, forma *albiflorus* (Burkart, 1935), but has not to my knowledge been cultivated.

L. tingitanus *(Linnaeus, 1753)*

The 'Tangier Pea' is a native of the Azores, Canaries, Portugal, Spain, Morocco, Algeria and Sardinia, but is widely naturalized elsewhere. It has been cultivated in Britain since 1680 and is very easy to grow. It can reach 3m tall and produces one to three bright purple flowers on a raceme that is 2–9cm long. Perhaps even more attractive is var. *roseus*, which has delightful pink flowers, though the origin of the name is obscure. 'Harmony' is alleged to be of hybrid origin but is indistinguishable from var. *roseus*. Rumours of a white-flowered variety occasionally emerge.

L. hirsutus *(Linnaeus, 1753)*

Also close to the Sweet Pea, the 'Caley Pea' is a native species of central and southern Europe and the western Mediterranean, spreading eastwards through northern Iran to Afghanistan. It is found in bushy and grassy places and cultivated land up

L. tingitanus 'Roseus'.

L. annuus 'Hotham Red'.

to 1880m altitude. It grows 0.2–1.2m high and produces one to three (rarely four) flowers per raceme, each 18–35mm across. The flowers are purple/lavender bicoloured. It is grown as a fodder crop in south-eastern states of the USA where it yields an abundant green mass that stays green for a long period. It is very easy to grow in the garden and can be grown as a meadow flower. It has been hybridized with *L. odoratus* and *L. cassius* under laboratory conditions.

L. annuus *(Linnaeus, 1753)*

Sometimes known as the 'Fodder Pea', this is a scrambling annual up to 1.5m tall. The type form was introduced into Britain in 1621 and it is extremely easy to cultivate. All fodder species are very suited to meadow cultivation. A number of forms have been described. Var. *annuus* is the typical form with one to three yellow flowers, each 12–18mm across, on a raceme up to 12cm long. It is native to the Mediterranean region, stretching westwards to the Canaries, Madeira and Azores and eastwards to Afghanistan. It is naturally found in scrub, hedges, water meadows, ditches, damp ground near sea and lakes, among rocks, cultivated and waste ground, orchards and roadsides up to 1200m altitude.

'Hotham Red' is a good variety with up to four red flowers per raceme. 'Mrs R. Penney' has

VARIETIES OF CHICKLING PEA

Seed size has sometimes been used to distinguish varieties but is an unreliable measure. The following varieties have been described:

- 'Albo-azuri'. An early, invalid name for the variety known as 'Blue Stripe'.
- var. *albus* (Alefeld, 1861), has lanceolate leaflets, 60–70mm × 6mm. Flowers are white. The legume is narrowly elliptic with one to four seeds.
- var. *azureus* (Korshinsky, 1898). As var. *cyaneus* except the flowers are pale blue, sometimes two per raceme.
- 'Blue Stripe'. Flowers white with a blue blotch on the standard.
- var. *coeruleus* (Alefeld, 1861), has linear-lanceolate leaflets 50mm × 5–6mm. The standard is pale blue, becoming pink towards the edges; wings are purple. The legume is broadly linear with three or four seeds.
- var. *coloratus* (Seringe, 1825), has lanceolate leaflets 60–70mm × 6mm. Flowers are white with blue veins; the wings white with large blotches of blue. The legume is broad elliptic with one to three, rarely four, seeds.
- var. *comitans* (Smekalova, 1991) is like var. *coloratus* except the standard is white; the wings are white with pale pinkish-blue blotches and pink centre.
- var. *cyaneus* (Howard and Khan, 1928), has narrowly linear leaflets 35–45mm × 3.5–4.5mm. The flowers are single, small and deep blue, the standard becoming purple at the edges. The legume normally has two or three seeds.
- var. *depressus* (Smekalova, 1991) is like var. *coloratus* except the standard is white with blue veins and sometimes spotted blue; the wings are blue.
- var. *pisiformis* (Smekalova, 1991) is like var. *coeruleus* except the standard is violet blue, becoming purple towards the edges; the wings are pink.
- var. *pulchrus* (Smekalova, 1991) is like var. *cyaneus* except the flowers are pink and red.
- 'Tutankhamun'. One of many trade names under which var. *azureus* is sometimes sold by seedsmen, on account of seeds of this species having been found in an ancient Egyptian tomb.
- var. *variegatus* (Smekalova, 1991) is like var. *coloratus* except the standard is white, heavily splashed with blue veins, spots and flecks, sometimes with a blue edge, sometimes spotted with pink; the wings are blue.

L. sativus var. *azureus*.

up to three orange flowers per raceme. Another form, var. *hierosolymitanus* (Post, 1896) has the synonym *L. hierosolymitanus* (Boissier, 1849) and is still regarded by some as a separate species. The 13mm-wide flowers are cream, sometimes tinged pink, and it is native to the eastern Mediterranean countries, and to Libya, where it is found in cornfields up to 500m altitude.

L. sativus *(Linnaeus, 1753)*

Very decorative and easy to grow is the 'Chickling Pea'. It has many common names in many languages but the recent trend to rename it as the Grass Pea is confusing since this name has traditionally been associated with *L. nissolia*. The Chickling Pea is of unknown origin but is widely naturalized in southern and central Europe, north Africa and southwest Asia. It is found on cultivated land, waste ground and roadsides. Very widely cultivated as fodder since ancient times, and sometimes as grain for human consumption, it can also be extremely poisonous and is the species most commonly associated with the sometimes fatal condition named 'Lathyrism'. An entire chapter could be written on the circumstances in which this is safe or unsafe to eat. It grows up to 1m high, rarely to 1.5m. Many varieties have been described but not many are in garden cultivation in the west.

L. clymenum *(Linnaeus, 1753)*

The 'Spanish Pea' is native to the Canaries, southern Portugal, south and east Spain, and the Mediterranean region. It is found on cultivated land, near water up to 350m altitude. It has been cultivated in Britain since 1640. It grows to 1m high and has racemes of one to six mauve/lavender bicoloured flowers, each 12mm across. It is very variable in the wild. The 'Jointed Pea', var. *articulatus* (Arcangeli, 1882), is considered by some to be a distinct species, *L. articulatus* (Linnaeus, 1753). However, so many different intermediate forms are found that this seems unlikely. This variety is native to Portugal and the Mediterranean

and has been grown in Britain since 1739. It differs from the type in its red/white bicoloured flowers. 'Chelsea' is a superior variety normally growing to 1.25m and with four to five pairs of leaflets. It has three to four mauve/lavender flowers, 16mm across, on 12.5cm-long racemes.

MEADOW FLOWERS

The increasing popularity of wild flower borders and meadow gardening provides an opportunity for climbing annuals to be naturalized in the garden and also provides an opportunity for many of the other true meadow annuals to be seen at their best, for example cream and yellow forms of the Yellow Vetchling, *L. aphaca*. There is hardly any *Lathyrus* which cannot be adapted to this style

L. pratensis.

of gardening but for some, such as the Grass Pea, *L. nissolia*, and the perennial Meadow Vetchling, *L. pratensis*, this is their natural environment. A good many of the species suitable for meadow gardening are delicate annuals with sometimes inconsequential red or purple flowers. They are not detailed in this chapter but are available from the National Collections for those who wish to try them.

SELF-SUPPORTING PERENNIALS

Members of this group are in some ways the easiest to grow since they are low perennials that require no support and most can be accommodated in any garden with good drainage. As woodland dwellers, they can suffer from a lack of shade in hot sunny weather. The Spring Pea, *L. vernus*, provides welcome blooms in early spring, followed by a decorative mound of green foliage to about 40cm (16in) high. It comes in various colour forms of which the pink and white bicolour is delightful among the yellows and blues of other plants so

commonly found as a colour at that time of year. This is followed by *L. aureus*, with brownish yellow flowers, and then *L. venetus* with attractive purple blooms. The later species flower, the taller they become until the climbing perennials are summer flowering. Self-supporting perennials generally fall into two categories: those with purple flowers and those with brownish-yellow flowers.

Brownish-yellow flowers

This is a complex of closely related species with brown to yellow-orange flowers. Difficulty in distinguishing them means that seeds and plants are sometimes distributed with the name incorrectly attributed.

L. aureus *(D. Brandza, 1883)*

This has also been distributed as *L. luteus*. It is native to Bulgaria, Greece, Romania, Crimea, Caucasia, north-west Turkey and northern Anatolia. Found in forest and scrub up to 2000m altitude, it grows up to 80cm tall and has two to

L. laevigatus.

twenty-five brown to yellow-orange flowers per raceme. It is distinguished from *L. laevigatus* by its leaflets (1.7 to 2.0 times longer than wide) and is distinguished from *L. gmelinii* by having a petiole 10–20mm long and with a 7–11cm raceme usually shorter than or as long as the leaves, containing flowers 15–20mm long. It has a simple tendril.

L. laevigatus *(Grenier, 1865)*

Native to Austria, Czechoslovakia, Yugoslavia, Poland, Romania and northern Ukraine, it is found in shady forests and among shrubs. It grows up to 70cm high and has three to seventeen yellowish flowers per raceme. It is distinguished from *L. aureus* by its leaflets 2.0 to 2.5 times longer than wide. It is distinguished from *L. gmelinii* by its leaflets and by its legume, which is 50–75mm × 5–8mm. It too has a simple tendril. It is reported to hybridize with *L. occidentalis* in the wild.

L. occidentalis *(Fritsch, 1895)*

This species may not be in cultivation. It is native to Spain, France, Germany, Switzerland, Austria, Italy, Yugoslavia and Romania. It grows up to 60cm high and has two to twenty yellow flowers per raceme. A very variable species from which many subspecies and forms have been described, it is said to be less hairy than *L. laevigatus*, with leaflets 3.3 to 6.0 times longer than wide and no tendril.

L. gmelinii *(Fritsch, 1895)*

Native to central and southern Urals and central Siberia, this is found in forests and forest meadows, rarely in alpine meadows. It grows to 1.5m high and has two to twenty brown to yellow-orange flowers per raceme. It is distinguished from *L. laevigatus* by its leaflets, which are 1.5 to 2.1 times longer than wide, and its legume is 60–80mm × 8–9mm. It is distinguished from *L. aureus* by having a petiole 21–25mm long and a raceme as long as or slightly longer than the leaves, containing flowers 25–30mm long. It has a simple tendril.

L. davidii (M. Thornhill).

L. transsylvanicus *(Reichenbach, 1885)*

Native to Czechoslovakia, Hungary, Romania and Russia, this grows to 60cm high and has two to twenty yellow flowers per raceme. Is very similar to *L. laevigatus* but has no tendril.

L. davidii *(Hance, 1871)*

This species grows to 1.2m tall. It has eight to twenty flowers on a raceme up to 15cm long, and flowers that start cream, becoming brownish orange. It is taller and later flowering than *L. aureus* and *L. laevigatus*. Tendrils are simple or branched. It is native to eastern Siberia, Manchuria, Ussuri, northern China, much of Japan, and Korea. It is found in woods and thickets on mountains, and in herbaceous slopes of dry hills. It was introduced into Britain in 1883. I have not personally seen the var. *roseus* (Chang, 2000), but presumably the flowers open with a pink tinge.

Purple flowers

L. vernus *(Bernhardi, 1800)*

Best known as the 'Spring Pea', this is the first to flower. It has sometimes been distributed in error as *L. alpestris* and *L. cyaneus*, neither of which are thought to be in cultivation. This species is native

L. vernus 'Albo-Roseus'.

VARIETIES OF SPRING PEA

- var. *albiflorus* (Ascherson and Graebner, 1909). Has white flowers and broad leaflets. Since botanists generally work from dried specimens, this is likely to be the very pale pink bicolour. Reports of 'true' white varieties arise from time to time but I have yet to see one.
- 'Albo-Roseus'. A name of obscure origin applied to var. *variegatus*, perhaps to avoid any misunderstanding over the leaf colour (AGM 1997).
- 'Albus'. Another name of obscure origin used for var. *albiflorus*. Plants with very pale flowers are not as strong as the deeper colours.
- forma *angustifolius* (Ascherson and Graebner, 1909). A narrow-leaved form of the type with mauve flowers and leaflets 3–5cm long and 6–15mm (rarely 5–18mm) wide. The stipules are never broader than the leaflets. Plants distributed in error as *L. alpestris* may be a selection of this form.
- 'Caeruleus'. A variety which was originally thought to be more blue than the type but is now inconsistent, perhaps as a result of reproducing it by seed.
- 'Cyaneus'. Another variety which was thought to be more blue than the type but now generally produces mixed plants from seed. Has been named the 'Blue Bitter Peavine' in the USA.
- subsp. *flaccidus* (Arcangeli, 1894). A naturally occurring subspecies with mauve flowers but leaflets longer and narrower than the type. The stipules are never narrower than the leaflets. Two forms occur: forma *flaccidus* with leaflets 4–12mm mm wide and forma *gracilis*.
- 'Flore Pleno'. A variety with double flowers, now thought to be lost.
- forma *gracilis* (Ascherson and Graebner, 1909). Mauve flowers and leaflets 1–2mm wide.
- 'Lamorna's Love'. A variety which appears to be consistently more blue than the type and has narrower leaflets.
- forma *macranthus* (Bassler, 1973). A naturally occurring form described as having larger flowers than the type, a character that may be unreliable.
- 'Praecox'. The name is unfortunate since it is no earlier than other Spring Peas. Very attractive, with pink/white bicoloured flowers and very narrow leaflets. Not as strong as broad leaf plants.
- 'Rosenelfe'. A good, slightly more compact, form of var. *variegatus*.
- var. *roseus* (Ascherson and Graebner, 1909). Pink flowers and broad leaflets. Seeds from a deeper pink/pale pink bicolour sold under this name may not come true.
- 'Spring Delight'. Thought to be a trade name for the typical species.
- 'Spring Melody'. Thought to be a trade name for var. *variegatus*.
- var. *variegatus* (Bassler, 1973). Pink/white bicolour and broad leaflets. The name is unfortunate since it refers to the variegated flowers, not the foliage, which is green.
- subsp. *vernus*. The typical species with mauve flowers and leaflets 15–25mm (rarely up to 35mm) wide (AGM 1993).

to Scandinavia, central Europe, the Balkans, Bulgaria, Romania, Russia, western and central Siberia, northern Anatolia, Caucasus and Iran. It is found in forests, scrub and rock ledges up to 1400m altitude.

The Spring Pea grows to 50cm high. It typically has racemes of three to fifteen mauve flowers, each 12–17mm across, and broad leaflets 3–5cm long. Many varieties of this easy and popular species can be found, some of which are distributed as hybrid plants and therefore do not come true from seed. They are all varying permutations of leaflet width and flower colour. Flower colours are basically mauve self, or pink/white bicolour. Flower colour changes with age so the type opens mauve, becoming more blue with age. Forms with paler wings are found, and some varieties are claimed to be more blue than the type, or consistently bicoloured, but on the whole this is unreliable. Some pink/white bicolours are very pale, fading to white, while some are very deep to give a deeper pink/pale pink bicolour.

L. venetus *(Wohlfarth in Koch, 1892)*

Native to central Europe, the Balkans, Bulgaria, Romania, central and southern Russia, and northen Anatolia, this species is found in forests and grazed land at 600m to 950m altitude. It grows to 40cm high and has six to thirty purple flowers per raceme. The plant is shorter than the Black Pea.

L. niger *(Bernhardi, 1800)*

The 'Black Pea' is native to Britain, Europe, Turkey, northern Iran, Syria, Corsica, Morocco and Algeria. It is found in forests, oak scrub and shady places up to 1000m altitude. It grows to 90cm high and has racemes of two to ten purple flowers, each 10–15mm wide. It flowers around the same time as *L. venetus* but is taller. The whole plant turns black once legumes form, making it useful for a black-themed planting scheme. Various forms have been described by botanists but are not in general cultivation.

L. linifolius in a pot.

L. linifolius *(Bassler, 1971)*

The 'Bitter Pea' is native to Europe, including Britain, Corsica and Algeria. It grows to 85cm high and has racemes of two to six mauve flowers, 10–16mm wide. A number of varieties have been described by botanists but are not in general cultivation. It is found in moist forests, woodland edges, hedges and scrub but enjoys good drainage in cultivation. By contrast, the Marsh Pea (below) does best, in my experience, in pots standing in a saucer of water.

L. palustris *(Linnaeus, 1753)*

Three subspecies are recognized, each with various forms within this very variable species. The 'Marsh Pea' is subsp. *palustris*, a native of Alaska, Canada, north-western USA, Iceland, Ireland, Britain and the rest of Europe, Corsica, from northern Turkey to Burma, Mongolia, Japan and Korea. It is found in marshy ground, tall damp grassland and scrub up to 1000m altitude. It grows to 1.2m high and has racemes of two to eight blue-purple flowers, each 12–20mm wide. The leaflets are six times longer than their width. The seeds are mottled red-brown.

Subsp. *pilosus* (O.E. Hulten, 1937) has a range stretching from western Russia through Siberia to Japan and Korea. It is found in wet grassy places in lowlands and grows up to 1.0m high. It has two to six lilac-blue flowers per raceme. The leaflets are three to five times longer than their width. The seeds are mottled red-brown.

Subsp. *nudicaulis* (P.W. Ball, 1968a) is a native of northern Portugal and northern Spain. It grows to 1.2m high and has two to eight bright red-purple flowers per raceme. The leaflets are six times longer than their width. The seeds are black.

L. neurolobus *(Boissier and Heldreich, 1849)*

Native to western Crete, this semi-evergreen perennial grows up to 0.5m long and is found in marshes, streams and springs, and moist shady rocks at 50m–300m altitude. It has one or two blue flowers, 9mm across, on a 20mm peduncle. Very easy to grow, it can be used on rock gardens where

L. neurolobus growing through rushes.

it forms a short compact plant, as a substitute for *Lobelia* in baskets and pots, or in the margins of ponds where growth is long and it climbs among rushes and other plants.

L. pisiformis *(Linnaeus, 1753)*

Native to Czechoslovakia, Hungary, Poland, western Russia, Caucasus, former Soviet central Asia, and western and central Siberia, this is found in mixed forests and forest edge among scrub, rarely on steppe meadows. It grows 1.0m high and has eight to fifteen (rarely up to twenty) red-purple flowers per raceme.

L. roseus *(Steven, 1813)*

This is not to be confused with pink-flowered varieties of other species. It grows to 1.5m and each raceme produces one to five magenta pink flowers, up to 25mm wide. It is native to Crimea, Caucasus, north and eastern Anatolia, and north and north-west Iran, and is found in forest and scrub to 1800m altitude.

ROCK GARDEN PLANTS

L. japonicus *(Willdenow, 1803)*

This perennial is better suited to the rock garden than the woodland garden since it is naturally found on maritime sands and shingle. There are two subspecies that are not easily distinguished, though leaflet size may help ordinary gardeners. Both are variable and widely distributed, including being naturalized throughout colder regions of the southern hemisphere.

Subsp. *japonicus*, the 'Beach Pea', is native to China, Japan, Korea, North America, Greenland, Iceland, northern Norway, Finland, and inland in north-west Russia and central Siberia. It grows up to 1.0m high and has 35–50mm-long racemes of two to twelve mauve flowers, each 10–25mm wide. It typically has leaflets twice as long as they are wide.

Subsp. *maritimus* (P.W. Ball, 1968) is the 'Sea Pea'. It is native to North America, Ireland, Britain, France, Germany, Scandinavia, Poland and western Russia, and is also found on maritime shingle and sand dunes. It grows up to 1.0m high and has 35–50mm long racemes of two to twelve (rarely fifteen) mauve flowers, each 15–25mm wide. The leaflets are 1.5 times as long as the width. This is the subspecies more likely to be encountered by UK gardeners. It has decorative flowers but requires very good drainage to grow well in the garden. A number of varieties have been described by botanists but are not

L. laxiflorus growing in a raised border.

in general cultivation, including var. *acutifolius* (Bassler, 1973), found in sand dunes of Angus and Shetland. It differs from subsp. *maritimus* in having narrower leaflets tapering at both ends.

L. laxiflorus *(Kuntze, 1887)*

Other rock garden plants include *L. laxiflorus*, the 'Hairy Bitter Pea' (plants have also been distributed under the obscure name *L. fremontii*). This species is native to southern Italy, Balkans, Crete, Bulgaria, western Russia, Turkey, north and north-west Iran, and Syria. It is found in margins of woodland and rocky places at up to 2000m altitude. It grows to 55cm tall and has one to six flowers, 10–20mm wide, on a raceme up to 8cm long. The flowers are mauve/lavender bicoloured. The leaflets are less than three times as long as they are wide, and the leaves occasionally end in a simple tendril. This is a variable species, such that several varieties have been described but are often mixed in the same population. A white-flowered form exists only in cultivation but has not yet been named or fixed. If cut back after flowering, this species should produce a second flush in mid-summer.

Subsp. *angustifolius* (P.H. Davis, 1970) is a form with leaflets more than three times as long as wide. The leaflets are usually narrower than the stipules, and the upper leaves usually end in tendrils.

Var. *glabratus* (Dinsmore, 1932) is native to northern Syria. Its plants are glabrescent, i.e. virtually without hairs, rather than the usual dense soft hairiness. This variety is not known to be in cultivation. Var. *rotundatus* (Kozhukharov, 1976) is native to Bulgaria. It has rounder leaflets and is probably not in cultivation.

L. magellanicus *(Lamarck, 1788)*

This species is occasionally found as *L. hookeri* (G. Don, 1832). The correct name has in the past been misapplied to the tall-growing *L. nervosus*. It is native to Chile, Argentina, Peruvian Andes, Ecuador, Colombia and Bolivia. It is a glaucous perennial up to 60cm high with racemes of three to seven mauve/lavender bicoloured, scented flowers, 14–26mm across.

L. multiceps *(Clos, 1846)*

Similar is this native of Argentina and Chile, found at 800m–2000m altitude. It has one to six scented, violet/white bicoloured flowers per raceme, which is up to 13cm long.

L. subandinus *(Philippi, 1862)*

This species is a native of Chile, found at 1800m–1850m altitude. It grows to 30cm tall and has six to fifteen violet blue/white bicoloured flowers per raceme.

L. multiceps.

These three very attractive South American species (above) may be better in pots than a rock garden and are not easy to grow. They may do better in the Scottish highlands than they do with me on the south coast of England.

CLIMBING PERENNIALS

Equally easy, but requiring support or room to sprawl, are the climbing perennials such as *L. latifolius*. This comes in various colour shades from deep magenta through to pink and white but does not always come true from seed. The group all have dense bushy foliage on vigorous growth and are useful for screening but the foliage dies back in winter. There are several related species that all provide blooms for cutting. All the European species have a long flowering period. The best is perhaps the Persian Everlasting Pea, *L. rotundifolius*, found in red and pink forms with foliage a little less coarse than the others.

L. latifolius *(Linnaeus, 1753)*

Best known is the common 'Everlasting Pea'. It is a native of central and southern Europe, stretching from Portugal to Crimea, and from France and Poland to Algeria and Morocco. It may be found in hedges, roadsides, railway banks, rough ground, forest edges and among shrubs. It has been widely

L. latifolius 'Wendy's Joy' (M. Thornhill).

VARIETIES OF EVERLASTING PEA

- forma *albiflorus* (Moldenke, 1973). A form with white flowers.
- 'Albus'. A superior variety with white flowers that has now deteriorated (AGM 1998).
- var. *angustifolius* (Koch, 1843). A natural variety with narrow leaflets and narrow legumes. Leaflets are 6–12mm wide and legumes 5–6mm wide.
- 'Appleblossom'. Appears to be a synonym for 'Blushing Bride'. Just to add to the confusion, the name has recently been applied by one seedsman to a variety of *L. odoratus*.
- 'Blushing Bride'. Flowers white flushed with pink. This name has also recently been applied to a variety of *L. odoratus*.
- 'Bridesmaid'. A trade name formerly used for *L. grandiflorus*.
- 'Pink Beauty'. Described as dark purple and red.

- 'Pink Pearl'. A synonym for 'Rosa Perle'.
- 'Red Pearl'. Flowers are magenta.
- 'Rosa Perle'. Flowers are pink (AGM 1997).
- 'Royal'. A synonym for 'Splendens'.
- 'Snow Queen'. A form with white flowers, thought to be a synonym of 'Albus'.
- 'Splendens'. A large-flowered variety that may still exist, described as having purple flowers. Not to be confused with the separate species *L. splendens*.
- 'Weisse Perle'. Originally a large-flowered white variety but inferior forms are now found under the name 'White Pearl' (AGM 1993).
- 'Wendy's Joy'. An excellent variety with mauve flowers.
- 'White Pearl'. A synonym for 'Weisse Perle'.

grown as a garden plant and is naturalized in many other parts of the world. The RHS awarded it an AGM in 1993. A vigorous perennial to 3m high, it produces three to twelve flowers, 15–30mm wide, per raceme in a range of colours during July to September. The leaflets are up to 50mm wide and the legumes are 6–10mm wide. This species forms a complex with *L. sylvestris* and *L. heterophyllus* that can be hybridized. It is very easy to grow and is used for cut flower production in some countries, although it is not as popular as Sweet Peas. As in *L. vernus*, the white form is not as strong as other colours. Variety names are confused since names have been applied to colours rather than the original, improved, true-breeding selection of a colour.

L. grandiflorus (*J. Sibthorp and J.E. Smith, 1813*)

The 'Two-flowered Pea' is sometimes confused with *L. latifolius* and the name has also led to confusion with the grandiflora type of Sweet Pea. This native of southern Italy, Sicily, southern Yugoslavia, Albania and Bulgaria was introduced into cultivation in Britain in 1814. In the wild it is found in shady places in the mountains. It grows

L. grandiflorus.

to 2m high and has one or two flowers per raceme. The flowers are the largest of any *Lathyrus* at 30–40mm wide and are an attractive pink/purple bicolour. It rarely produces seed but spreads by underground stolons so is usually only available to buy as a plant. It is very easy to grow but is not reliably hardy.

L. sylvestris *(Linnaeus, 1753)*

The 'Narrow-leaved Everlasting Pea' is native to Europe, the Canaries, Morocco, Palestine, Turkey and eastwards to Afghanistan. Found in scrub, woodland edge, hedges and rough ground, it grows to 2m tall with three to twelve pink/purple bicoloured flowers, 12–20mm wide, on a 6–20cm long raceme. It appears closer to *L. heterophyllus* than to *L. latifolius*. The traditional distinction from *L.latifolius* of leaflet width is no longer reliable since broad-leaved plants with *L. sylvestris* flowers are known and narrow-leaved plants with *L. latifolius* flowers are known. It is a good nectar plant.

L. heterophyllus *(Linnaeus, 1753)*

A native of Sweden, Portugal, Spain, France, Germany, Poland, Switzerland, Austria, Czechoslovakia, Sardinia and Italy, this species grows to 3m high and has racemes of five to fifteen purple-pink flowers, 12–22mm wide. It has been hybridized with *L. latifolius*. Normally it has multijugate leaves but the form commonly grown in the UK is var. *unijugus* (C. Stace 1991), known as the 'Norfolk Everlasting Pea' – a native of west Norfolk where it is found in damp hollows of coastal dunes. This unijugate form is very similar to *L. sylvestris* but has stipules 30–60mm long by 2–11mm wide. The legume is 8.3 to 11 times longer than the width.

L. rotundifolius *(Willdenow, 1802)*

Known as the 'Persian Everlasting Pea', this is a delightful species, more refined than the common Everlasting Pea, though a little less robust. It received an AGM in 2002. It grows up to 2.5m

L. rotundifolius.

high and produces four to twelve red or pink, 14–21mm-wide flowers per 2.5–8.cm-long raceme. It is native to Crimea, Caucasia and E. Turkey, and neighbouring areas of Iraq and Iran where it is found in pine forest and oak scrub. There is a subspecies *miniatus* (P.H. Davis, 1970), which is probably not in cultivation. 'Tillyperone' is a selection compatible with the natural variation within the species. A hybrid with *L. tuberosus*, named *L.* × *tubro*, exhibits mostly *L. rotundifolius* characteristics.

L. tuberosus *(Linnaeus, 1753)*

This is known as the 'Fyfield Pea'. It occurs in most of Europe, western Siberia, Turkey, the former Soviet central Asia, Iraq, and western Iran. Found in water meadows, steppes, grassy banks, fallow fields, cornfields, hedges and roadsides up to 2150m altitude, it grows to 1.2m high and has two to nine mauve pink, 9–20mm wide flowers on racemes up to 50mm long. The tubers are edible and allegedly nutty flavoured, though I have never been tempted to try them.

L. cirrhosus *(Seringe, 1825)*

A native of the Pyrenees and Cevennes, it has been cultivated in Britain since 1870. It grows 0.9–1.2m high and has four to ten rose pink flowers per raceme. Flowers from June to August and survives well in a hot dry border. A fine compact grower.

Two very exotic climbing perennials proving hardy in sheltered southern gardens during most winters are *L. pubescens* and Lord Anson's Pea, *L. nervosus*. Both are from South America and have large racemes of violet blue flowers but differ in their foliage. On hot, still days they are strongly scented.

L. nervosus *(Lamarck, 1788)*

This is well known as 'Lord Anson's Pea'. It is a native of Argentina, Chile, Uruguay, Brazil, Ecuador and Colombia. Prefers cool moist air. Is occasionally hardy in the UK and generally flowers in the third year on the south coast of England. This species is a glaucous evergreen perennial

L. nervosus.

climbing to 2m with conspicuous hastate stipules and very thick, leathery leaflets. It has three to ten violet blue flowers on a long raceme.

L. pubescens *(W.J. Hooker and Arnott, 1831)*

Native to Argentina, Chile, Paraguay, Uruguay, Brazil and Bolivia, this is a variable species but the form in cultivation is a perennial climber to 3m with six to sixteen violet blue flowers per raceme. The stipule is semi-sagittate. It has one pair of leaflets and branched tendrils. The green hairy leaflets are elliptic-lanceolate, 25–75mm × 5–15mm. The flowers are similar to *L. nervosus* but the vegetative parts are very distinct.

NORTH AMERICAN SPECIES

There are many species endemic to North America which are decorative and occasionally encountered in cultivation. It might be thought that they should be more widely grown but they have proved difficult to maintain as garden plants, even in North America. Many live in harsh climatic conditions and require extremely good drainage. Some are very localized in their natural distribution so obtaining seeds is unlikely. The following may be encountered in cultivation in the UK.

L. polyphyllus *(Nuttall in Torrey and Gray, 1838)*

The 'Oregon Pea' is native to northern California coast ranges through to Puget Sound, Washington State and is found in mountains and prairies. A self-supporting perennial, it grows to 0.4–1.0m high. It has five to thirteen flowers, conspicuously one-sided on each raceme. The flowers are mauve/lavender bicoloured.

L. splendens *(Kellogg, 1876)*

The 'Pride of California' is not to be confused with *L. latifolius* 'Splendens'. This species is rarely encountered in cultivation but is very desirable. It is difficult to cultivate even in California, requiring good drainage and summer drought. Distributed from San Diego county, California, south to Baja (Mexico), it is found in desert, mountain woodland on dry north-facing slopes, dry roadsides and clambering through woody shrubs on rocky sandy loams. A climbing perennial with woody haulm up to 3m long, it has the most wonderful dark crimson flowers with elongated, reflexed standard petals.

L. vestitus *(Nuttall in Torrey and Gray, 1838)*

A variable species with changing taxonomic status because of the number of subspecies that have been described. They are climbing perennials, perhaps growing taller in cultivation than they are found in the wild. The two forms in my National Collection are thought to be subsp. *vestitus* (the 'Pacific Pea') and subsp. *alefeldii* (the 'San Diego Pea'). Subsp. *vestitus* is native to Oregon and California where it is found in coastal scrub and woods. Each raceme bears up to twenty flowers. It is variable in colour but the form we have has a pink standard and white wings. Subsp. *alefeldii* (Broich, 1987), the 'San Diego Pea', is also found as *L. alefeldii* (T.G. White, 1894). It is native to California and has mauve blue flowers.

L. lanszwertii *(Kellogg, 1863)*

The 'Nevada Pea' is not known to be in cultivation. Plants and seeds distributed under this name have proved to be *Vicia Americana* (Willdenow, 1802).

Of all the species described, some are very easy to grow while some present a challenge for the determined gardener. They can be very useful for a wide variety of locations in the garden but it is inconceivable that any will supplant the Sweet Pea as one of the world's most popular flowers.

L. vestitus.

Acknowledgements

This book is dedicated to my wife, Alison, without whose love, support and patience I would not have achieved anything. Her contribution to this book has included reading a first draft and in doing lots of jobs I should have been doing instead of writing.

Many Sweet Pea friends have been a source of inspiration and knowledge to me over the years, but I would especially like to thank Keith Hammett from New Zealand who has long been most generous in an informal mentoring role and supporter of my National Collection. Kaoru Nakamura from Japan has been a more recent friend, giving me some insight on the immense body of knowledge on Sweet Peas that exists in his country. Closer to home, David Guscott of Greenlines Nursery has given me detailed insight into commercial crop production, the world of real horticulture.

Other friends from the National Sweet Pea Society (NSPS) whose knowledge and experience I have soaked up over the years are too numerous to mention, but I am grateful to all for their friendship and support. Photographs in this book are my own or from the NSPS archives except where individually credited.

Glossary of Botanical Terms

Androecium: A collective term for all the stamens in a flower.

Anther: The pollen-bearing portion of the stamen.

Axil: The angle formed by a leaf with the shoot.

Calyx: A whorl of modified leaves that separates to release the flower.

Carpel: The ovule-bearing organ of the flower. Seeds will develop from the fertilized ovules.

Cleistogamous: A flower that self-fertilizes without the need to open.

Cotyledon: The embryonic leaves arising from the seed.

Cultivar: A variety arising from cultivation not found in wild populations.

Dehiscent: Describes a legume, or other seed capsule, that twists open on ripening.

Determinate: Growth of plant shoots which is limited during the growing season when cell division ceases at the shoot tip. The opposite of indeterminate.

Duplex: In the context of Sweet Peas, a flower with two standard petals.

Elliptic: Used here to describe the shape of a leaflet where the widest point is midway along the length and the edges are symmetrically curved.

Filament: The stalk that supports the stamen.

Funiculus: The stalk that attaches the developing seed to the legume.

Genus: A group of closely related species. The taxonomic rank above a species but below a family. *Lathyrus* is a genus of about 160 species.

Glaucous: Smooth or hairless, usually associated with a blue-green colour.

Gynoecium: A collective term for all the carpels in a flower. In *Lathyrus* there is only one carpel.

Hastate: Like an arrow head but with the basal lobes pointing outwards nearly at right-angles.

Haulm: The vegetative parts of the plant, excluding roots and flowers / legumes.

Hilum: The funicular scar on a seed coat.

Hybridization: Cross-breeding of two distinct plants (varieties, species, etc.) to produce a new plant.

Hypocotyl: The embryonic stem arising from a seed, located below the cotyledon.

Indehiscent: Describes a legume, or other seed capsule, that does not twist open on ripening.

Indeterminate: Continual growth of plant shoots which is not limited. The opposite of determinate.

Lanceolate: Lance-shaped i.e. much longer than wide, broader at or above the base and tapering to the apex.

Legume: A dry fruit derived from one carpel that splits along two sutures.

Mycorrhiza: A beneficial fungus found associated with plant roots.

Multiflora: In the context of Sweet Peas, a raceme with five or more flowers.

Multijugate: A leaf containing two or more pairs of leaflets.

Mutation: A genetic change which, when transmitted to offspring, gives rise to heritable variation.

Node: The point on a shoot where leaves are attached, or where a shoot branches.

Ovate: Egg-shaped, i.e. the widest point is below midway along the length and the edges are symmetrically curved.

Paripinnate: A pinnate leaf with an even number of leaflets and no terminal leaflet.

Pauciflora: In the context of Sweet Peas, a raceme with four or less flowers.

Pedicel: The individual flower stalk.

Peduncle: The main stalk for an entire inflorescence.

Petiole: A leaf stalk.

Pinnate: A compound leaf with leaflets arranged on both sides of the mid-rib.

Raceme: An unbranched, indeterminate inflorescence with pedicelled flowers.

Semisagittate: Sagittate means arrow-shaped but with the basal lobes pointing downwards. Semisagittate is this shape divided length-ways.

Simplex: In the context of Sweet Peas, a flower that has a single standard i.e. normal flower form.

Species: A fundamental category of naturally-occurring plants whose individuals have the potential to freely breed with one another and that is distinct from other species. The taxonomic rank above a subspecies but below a genus.

Stamen: The pollen-bearing structure.

Stenonychioid: A petal with tissue contracting into a narrow claw and with no distinct constriction between the petal and the claw.

Stigma: The pollen-receiving structure.

Stipule: A pair of structures at the base of the petiole. In *Lathyrus*, stipules are either hastate or semisagittate in shape.

Stolon: A propagative shoot that roots at the tip to produce a new plant.

Style: The structure that transfers pollen from the stigma to the carpel.

Subspecies: A subdivision of a species whose members have certain characteristics that distinguish them from other populations within the species.

Synonym: Any one of two or more names applied to a species or cultivar. Usually applied to the name that should be rejected as having been misapplied.

Unijugate: A leaf containing one pair of leaflets.

Further Reading

Many books have been written about Sweet Peas, providing an invaluable record of the flower's development. A particularly useful source of contemporary information is the Sweet Pea Annual, published by NSPS every year since 1905, apart from three years during World War 2. See also the following.

CHAPTER 1

Dicks, S.B. 'Early history of the Sweet Pea' in *1922 Sweet Pea Annual* :22–26 NSPS

Parsons, R. 'Early history of the Sweet Pea' in C. Ball (ed.) *National Sweet Pea Society Centenary Celebration 1900–2000* :5–19 NSPS. This contains a referenced account on which most of this chapter is based.

CHAPTER 2

Curtis, C.H. & Eckford, J.S. 'Evolution of the Sweet Pea' in R. Dean (ed.) *The Sweet Pea Bicentennary Celebration* :23-31 NSPS

Cuthbertson, F. in L.L. Morse (ed.) *Field Notes on Sweet Peas* (C.C. Morse & Co., San Francisco)

Dicks, S.B. 'More Historical Notes' in *1908 Sweet Pea Annual* :12–15 NSPS

Fraser, D.D. *Sweet Peas: How to grow the perfect flower* (Amalgamated Press, London)

Hammett, K. 'Early-flowering Sweet Pea strains' in C. Ball (ed.) *National Sweet Pea Society Centenary Celebration 1900–2000* :23–32 NSPS

Parsons, R. 'Early history of the Sweet Pea' in C. Ball (ed.) *National Sweet Pea Society Centenary Celebration 1900–2000* :5–19 NSPS

Unwin, C. 'The Zvolaneks' in *1971 Sweet Pea Annual* :86–87 NSPS

CHAPTER 3

Harrod, S. 'The mechanism of malformation' in C. Ball (ed.) *National Sweet Pea Society Centenary Celebration 1900–2000* :90–105 NSPS

Kupicha, F.K. 'The infrageneric structure of *Lathyrus*' Notes RBG Edinburgh 41(2):209–244

CHAPTER 7

Smith, S.E.G. *Enjoy Sweet Peas* (NSPS)

CHAPTER 8

Poulter, R., Harvey, L. & Burritt, D.J. 'Qualitative resistance to powdery mildew in hybrid sweet peas' *Euphytica* 133: 349–358

CHAPTER 11

Pockley, D. 'The Busby Sweet Peas' in T. North (ed.) *Australian Garden Journal* 2(7): 123

Index

OTHER GARDENING TITLES FROM CROWOOD

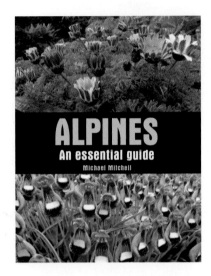

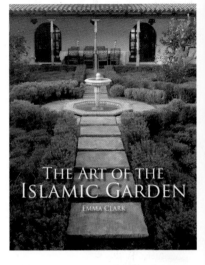

Alpines – An Essential Guide
ISBN 978 1 84797 295 8

A Gardener's Guide to
Snowdrops
ISBN 978 1 78500 449 0

The Art of the Islamic Garden
ISBN 978 1 84797 204 0

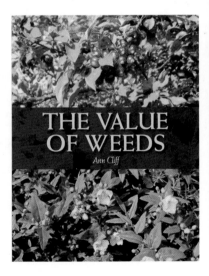

Cacti and Succulents
ISBN 978 1 86126 872 3

Garden Plants for
Mediterranean Climates
ISBN 978 1 86126 895 2

The Value of Weeds
ISBN 978 1 78500 278 6

www.crowood.com